Sharpe's VICTORY

This is an updated edition of *Sharpe's Story*, first published in hardback in 1996
This updated and expanded edition published by Carlton Books 1997
Design copyright © Carlton Books Limited 1996 & 1997. Text copyright ©Rachel Murrell 1996 & 1997

ISBN 1 85868 286 X

Executive Editors: Lorraine Dickey & Julian Flanders
Art Direction: Russell Porter
Book Design: Diane Klein
Project Editor: Lol Henderson
Production: Sarah Schuman

Photographs © Carlton Television Ltd
Map illustrations on pages 126, 142 and 143 by Geoff Fowler, with reference to Chandler D.G., *Dictionary of the Napoleonic Wars*, Greenhill Books, 1993 and *"The Hundred Days Waterloo, 1915"*, John Barratt, Partizan Books, 1992.

Printed and bound in Spain

ACKNOWLEDGEMENTS
The publishers would like to thank the photographer, Tony Nutley, and costume designer John Mollo for the use of his pictures. The publishers would also like to thank the following artistes who appear in the photographs: Simon Andreu, Philip Anthony, Jayne Ashbourne, Feódor Atkine, Edward Atterton, Sean Bean, Paul Bettany, Nigel Betts, Allie Byrne, Michael Byrne, Kirill Chevkine, Michael Cochrane, Brian Cox, Abigail Cruttenden, Lyndon Davies, Philip Dowd, Julian Fellowes, Hugh Fraser, Philip Glenister, Francois Guetary, Tony Haygarth, Nolan Hemmings, Douglas Henshall, Elizabeth Hurley, John Kavanagh, Alice Krige, Caroline Langrishe, James Laurenson, Michael Mears, Emily Mortimer, Gavan O'Herlihy, Daragh O'Malley, Cecile Paoli, Robert Patterson, Diana Perez, Berrin Politi, Pete Postlethwaite, James Purefoy, Jason Salkey, Matthew Scurfield, Assumpta Serna, Ian Shaw, Mark Strong, John Tams, Paul Trussell, Philip Whitchurch, and all stuntmen and extras.

While every effort has been made to trace artistes featured photographically in this book, Carlton Television Ltd and the publishers will be glad to make proper acknowledgement in future editions of this publication in the event that any regrettable omissions have occurred by the time of going to press.

The author would like to thank the following people for their kind assistance: Ali Akdeniz, Jayne Ashbourne, Feódor Atkine, Sean Bean, Chris Burt, Ted Childs, Tom Clegg, Bernard Cornwell, Malcolm Craddock, Sam Craddock, Gina Cronk, Abigail Cruttenden, Lyndon Davies, Pavel Douvidson, John Raymond, Julian Fellowes, Dennis Firminger, Eoghan Harris, Katherine Hedderly, John Hubbard, Morgan Jones, Alex Košević, Simon Lewis, Michael Mears, Caroline McManus, Irene Meldris, Andrew Mollo, Igor Nossov, Daragh O'Malley, Diana Perez, Stepan Pojenian, Pete Postlethwaite, Dinny Powell, Julian Putkowski, Hugh Ross, Jason Salkey, Assumpta Serna, Tatyana Shakhgeldyan, Ivan Strasburg, Muir Sutherland, Colin Thurston, Christian Wangler, William J Whitelaw and Cindy Winter. Special thanks to John Mollo for his pictures, John Tams, Richard Rutherford Moore and John Murrell.

VICTORY

THE STORY OF A HERO'S TRIUMPH

RACHEL MURRELL

CARLTON

CONTENTS

Sharpe's Comrades

*Sharpe himself, the men who fought alongside him, those
who fought against him, and the women he loved - as seen by
the actors and actresses themselves.*

S E A N   B E A N   a s

Sharpe

ou did me a damn good turn. Now I'm going to do you a damn bad one. I'm giving you a field commission. From this moment on, you're a lieutenant in the 95th.'

With these words, Sir Arthur Wellesley – soon to be the Duke of Wellington – rewards Richard Sharpe for saving his life by plucking him from the ranks and making him an officer, changing at a stroke the whole course of his life. From then on, Sharpe is an outsider. His fellow officers sneer at him because he is not a gentleman, and his men mistrust him because he is no longer one of them. Only in battle is he at his ease. And in battle, he is magnificent. His courage, strength and determination to win mark him out as a man Wellington can make use of.

Richard Sharpe was born in the late 1770s, the son of a whore. He spent his childhood in orphanages and workhouses, fighting, stealing and cheating to stay alive. When he killed a man to defend a friend, Sharpe became a fugitive from the law. And, like thousands of others before him, he joined the army.

He enlisted in the 33rd Regiment, serving in India – spending three months as a prisoner of the Tippoo Sultan before escaping and killing his captors – and then getting posted to Portugal at the beginning of the Peninsular War. During the long hard winter of 1808-09, Sharpe was one of a small group of riflemen cut off from the rearguard of Sir John Moore's army in the retreat to Còruna. He was later part of a stronger, better-equipped force which returned to drive Napoleon's forces from Spain.

It was then that fate took a hand in his advancement. Sharpe saved Wellington's life – in the novels, this happens at the battle of Assaye in

Sharpe and (from left) Cooper, Tongue, Hagman, Perkins, Harris and Harper

India, but in the film *Sharpe's Rifles*, it happens in Spain – earning promotion and regular work as Wellington's troubleshooter.

The army is Sharpe's world. He abides by its harsh rules, but if those same rules conflict with natural justice, he's prepared to break them. Although he loves the army for its values of honour and decency, he also hates it for allowing the wealthy and the well-born to buy their way to power and influence over better men.

Sharpe's innate sense of justice often gets him into trouble, notably in India, where he reported a sadistic sergeant – Obadiah Hakeswill – for torturing a man, and ended up accused of the atrocity himself. Hakeswill had Sharpe flogged and the resulting feud underlies events in *Sharpe's Company* and is pursued to the death in *Sharpe's Enemy*.

Sharpe's first command is of a small group of riflemen in the 95th known as the Chosen Men. Initially he comes down hard on them for their sloppy conduct and shabby appearance, but learns a less authoritarian approach from Comandante Teresa, the Spanish partisan, leading by example rather than ruling by force. Teresa also teaches Sharpe to love, and despite frequent partings and the constant fear of losing each other to a bullet or a knife, they develop an enduring relationship and have a daughter, Antonia.

With Teresa, Sharpe can reveal his vulnerable side, but in public he is moody and in frequent conflict with his superiors. His manner, his proud insistence on wearing the uniform of a rifleman rather than that

Lt. Richard Sharpe: courage, strength and determination

At first an authoritarian, Sharpe learns to lead by example

of an officer, and the scars of his flogging mean that he is sometimes taken for an ordinary soldier.

It's a mistake people do not make twice. They quickly learn that Sharpe was not born to his commission, nor did he buy it. He earnt it. And a man raised from the ranks is a force to be reckoned with.

In the books, Sharpe is a dark-haired cockney, but since Sean Bean took on the role, the character has become inseparable in the public mind from a fair-haired, athletic South Yorkshireman.

Two things strike you about that Yorkshireman when you first meet him. The first is that he's quiet, serious and almost shy. He speaks with the accent of his native Sheffield, and it's no secret that he's happier in the pub with his mates than at a showbiz event – or being interviewed.

The second is his smile. You get so used to seeing Sean onscreen as an evil villain or a stern-faced hero that when he smiles – it's as if a light has come on in the room.

Sean and Sharpe have a lot in common. Both are tough, working class lads with the ambition to make something of themselves. And both achieved it. Sean left school at 16 and went into an apprenticeship in his father's welding shop. After four years, he decided to go to art college in Rotherham, but it wasn't until he took some drama classes that he realised where his true vocation lay: 'Once I'd decided what I wanted to do, I got really into it,' he says. 'I was reading books and plays and going to the theatre and everything. I couldn't get enough.'

Sean was half-way through a two year course when he was accepted by RADA. He jokes about it now: 'RADA was the only place I applied to because I didn't think there were any more. That's how green I was.'

He's come a long way since then, specialising in screen villains in *Patriot Games*, *Scarlett*, *Clarissa*, *Fool's Gold* and, of course, the latest Bond film, *GoldenEye*. He played Mellors in *Lady Chatterley*, Theresa

Russell's married lover in *A Woman's Guide To Adultery*, and a host of other film and TV roles. But fame didn't happen overnight. Sean's first job was in *Romeo and Juliet* at the Water Mill, Newbury, and he has spent five years in theatre, all told, including a spell with the RSC.

Throughout his career, Sean has done all his own stunts, and has been injured as a result. 'You put yourself out on a limb occasionally,' says Sean. 'But I enjoy doing it, it's part of the job. And it always looks better.'

Sean's very fit, and has a particular talent for swordplay, which he studied intensively at RADA and for which he won prizes. On *Sharpe*, he got extra coaching in fencing from a Russian Olympic champion. 'He was fantastic to watch,' says Sean. 'Such poise and grace. You learn things from people like that. There's been many good fights. The fight with Jason Durr in *Sharpe's Battle*, that was a good fight. I got a few stitches in my hand from that.'

He's had worse. 'I got smacked across the face with wooden pole by Harrison Ford in *Patriot Games*,' he says. 'It was an accident. He gave me two black eyes, bashed my nose, and I had ten stitches in my eye.'

But even that had its up-side: 'We used the scar over my eye for *Sharpe*,' says Sean. 'We make it up a bit more and it looks great.'

But Sean's not just an all-action hero. He enjoys bringing out Sharpe's emotional side from time to time and, having played his share of sex scenes in other shows, values the fact that in *Sharpe* the love scenes are romantic rather than erotic. The recent films see Sharpe meet a new love: '*Regiment* is when I meet Jane Gibbons, and fall in love with her,' says Sean. 'I eventually get married to her during *Siege*. The marriage goes its own way, but a relationship is formed which is quite interesting, because in the last few episodes, it's been like a girl every week, y'know what I mean?' In *Sharpe's Revenge*, Sharpe falls in love with Lucille, a young French widow. At first, mindful of his marriage vows, he tries to resist her. But when Jane takes a lover, Sharpe finally succumbs.

In real life, Sean's two daughters are among his biggest fans.

'Lorna's watched all the *Sharpe* films,' says Sean, 'and now Molly's started. They watch 'em when I'm away. They like it cos I'm the boss, know what I mean? I'm going round telling everybody what to do, and they can say, "That's my dad".'

Sheffield's most famous son may have lived in London for more than 15 years, but he still makes frequent visits home to see a large and loyal crowd of friends.

'It's always nice to go back home and get your feet on the ground,' he says. 'They always treat me like the person they grew up with, went to school with, or go to the match with. That's the

Sean Bean: an all-action hero who knows his Bond from his Bard

beauty of going back home. I can relax. Be myself.'

And although ambitious, Sean has never been a starry actor: 'I do my job and that's about it really,' he says. 'I concentrate on doing the best quality work that I can, and doing justice to that work. Anything above that is not of too much concern to me.'

What does concern him, however, is Sheffield United – and he has the words '100% Blade' tattooed on his arm to prove it. On more than one occasion, this passion has nearly interfered with Sean's acting career. Once he got back from a match with 10 minutes to spare before he had to go on stage.

'Sheffield United were playing Leeds United at Elland Road,' remembers Sean with a smile, 'I was playing Romeo in *Romeo and Juliet*, and I arrived ten minutes before curtain went up. Luckily it was a modern day production by Michael Bogdanov, so I just chucked my suit on, put my hair back and went on'

There was another incident a few years later when a match in London ended up in a good-natured pitch invasion. Sean had already joined the flood of fans going onto the pitch before he remembered he was due to fly to the US the following day to begin work on *Patriot Games*. He had to dodge a few police officers and hope he didn't get arrested so that he could make his flight. He laughs at the memory: 'It was a jubilant thing, not a nasty one, after the game had finished,' he says. Then he adds mischievously, 'Anyway, by going across the pitch you got to the tube station a lot quicker.'

When Sean was in the Ukraine filming *Sharpe*, he often called home for news of a big match, and more than once he'd spend a full 90 minutes glued to the telephone listening to a radio at the other end.

Small wonder, then, that when producer Jimmy Daly offered him the lead in *When Saturday Comes*, a film about Sheffield United, he jumped at the chance. 'I couldn't have picked a better part for myself,' says Sean. 'In fact, I thought it was a wind-up at first. Jimmy rang me up, he said "I'm making a film about Sheffield United", and I thought "Oh aye, this is one of my mates winding me up. Who is it this time?"'

But Sean rang Jimmy back a few weeks later, and the resulting film – which also stars Pete Postlethwaite – premiered in Sheffield in Spring 1996.

The future is full of promise. Sean is in discussion on a number of future projects, among them a film of Sharpe's adventures in India called *Sharpe's Tiger* and a TV version of *The Prisoner of Zenda*.

Sean is also keen to work on the other side of the camera. He's currently developing another project with Pete Postlethwaite and Jimmy Daly, only this time, as well as starring in it, he'll be one of its producers.

'I've been on this side of the fence for the last ten, twelve years,' says Sean. 'I've been around with actors with crews, so I know what goes on. But I like to know about things like that. I think it's good for everybody to know a little bit about what's happening.'

Like Richard Sharpe, Sean Bean is an ambitious man. And like Sharpe, you have a feeling he'll fight until he's got what he wants.

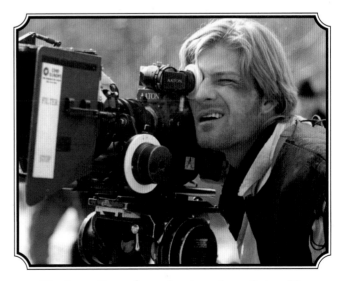

Restless ambition: Sean plans to produce a feature film

DARAGH O'MALLEY as

Patrick Harper

Daragh O'Malley plays Sgt. Harper, the huge and fearless Irishman who is Sharpe's second in command

aragh O'Malley is one of the longest-serving members of the *Sharpe* team. He was cast in the role of Sgt. Patrick Harper seven years ago, before the leading man – and even the director. As the veteran of some 85 weeks filming *Sharpe* in the last five years, Daragh has seen the project nearly fall apart more than once, and no-one is more surprised than he that the films are now in their fifth series.

For Daragh, it began back in 1989 in a Dublin bar. 'I knew Kenny [Mc Bain] from my drama school days when he was starting off in London. I bumped into him in a bar one night and he said "I'm here casting this thing called *Sharpe*, and y'know, I don't think there's anything in it for you because you're too young to play the role of Harper". Anyway, he was meeting Eoghan Harris, the writer, and when Eoghan came in, he took one look at me and said "Jaysus, Kenny, he's perfect for this".'

The first set-back came early on. Central decided to pull the plug, and soon afterwards, Kenny died. 'I thought that would be the end of *Sharpe*,' says Daragh.

Three years later, he got a phone call saying the project was up and running again, was he still interested in playing Harper? He was, and after new screen-tests for Sharpe, Daragh was in the Ukraine with Paul McGann in the leading role.

The second disaster came two days into filming. Paul injured his knee, and cast and crew came home. Once again, Daragh thought the show would collapse.

Fortunately, he was wrong. In less than a week, he was back in the Ukraine, playing the big, brawny Irish fellow – this time opposite Sean Bean.

Patrick Harper grew up in a small village in Donegal. The fourth of eleven children, he was permanently hungry, and he left home at 16 to go to Derry to seek his fortune. After a night on the juice, he woke up to find he'd joined the British Army.

From that moment, though he is a brave and fearless soldier in the service of King George, not a day goes by when he doesn't long for home. And there is the question of loyalty: how can a red-blooded Irishman fight in the ranks of the same army that is rampaging across his own land?

Thousands of his compatriots faced the same problem. But hunger forces hard choices, and the British army offered a job, comradeship and a role in life. If Harper sometimes wonders what it will be like, after years of fighting for the English, to go home where they are the enemy, he is not alone. In some regiments, as many as 40% of the men were Irish and orders were often given in Gaelic.

Harper and Sharpe fight side by side, watching each other's backs and frequently saving each other from death. When Sharpe is injured, it is Harper who nurses him back to health. When he's captured, Harper leads the rescue party. The two men share danger and booty in equal parts, and Harper makes Sharpe's enemies his own with no questions asked.

It wasn't always so. When they first meet in *Rifles*, Harper and his new lieutenant get off to a bad start. Harper recognises that Sharpe is not a gentleman, and resents being under the command of a man no better than himself. A fight breaks out. But after a struggle in which Sharpe fights as dirty as any London ruffian, and an altercation with some rebel Spaniards in which Harper proves his loyalty, the two men begin to work together.

Over time, and despite their difference in rank, this matures into the friendship which is at the core of the *Sharpe* films. According to Daragh, *Rifles* is in some ways a male love story.

One rare occasion when this friendship comes under threat was in

Friends as well as comrades, Sharpe and Harper fight side by side, sharing danger and watching each other's backs

the film *Sharpe's Battle*, when news of British atrocities in Ireland forces Harper to confront his own divided loyalties. But he places loyalty to his comrade above loyalty to country, and when Sharpe asks, 'You'll stay with me, Pat?', Harper replies – as if it was never in question – 'I always do.'

These are two very different men. Sharpe is ambitious and vengeful: quick to take offence, he fights to confirm his own worth. Harper has a different goal, he fights for a living. He has some money put aside, and a mother he loves in Donegal; the quicker they win this war, the quicker he can get home to Ireland.

They also differ in their attitudes to love. Harper is faithful to Ramona (Diana Perez), the Portuguese camp-follower with whom he has a child, and according to Daragh, mildly disapproves of Sharpe's less constant approach to women. So when Sharpe presses him to marry Ramona, Harper is quite taken aback. 'He felt like saying, who the hell are you to tell me to marry her?', says Daragh. In fact, his reluctance is not because he doesn't love Ramona, but because marrying her would hurt his mother's feelings.

Daragh gives his all in the action scenes, but doesn't share Sean's love of stunts: 'Hold on, is this gun going to go off in my face?'

Harper and Ramona with son Patrick Jose Hagman Cooper
Harris Perkins Harper - named after the midwives

Such sensitivity is typical of Harper. Although willing to follow Sharpe's lead on tactical matters, in the sphere of emotions, he is by far the more perceptive of the two.

Although Daragh looks in his element on a bloodstained battlefield, something of that sensitivity is evident in him too.

'Sean enjoys the action scenes, and Jason loves pulling people off horses, or jumping over something. But with me it's, 'Hold on a second. Is this gun going to go off in my face?'

Daragh grew up in Limerick in Ireland. He studied at the London Academy of Music and Dramatic Arts, and soon landed a role in *Crossroads*. He filmed 167 episodes as the gardener, Pat Grogan, many of them with another Irishman, Stephen Rea, who played the chef.

After a string of roles in films directed by Stephen Frears, Pat O'Conner, Bruce Robinson and others, Daragh gave up acting to co-run an actors' agency in Dublin. Since *Sharpe*, Daragh has been cast in *Divine Rapture*, the Marlon Brando film which sadly collapsed in the summer of 1995.

The Chosen Men

n the films, Sharpe and Harper are accompanied by a select group of hand-picked riflemen known as the Chosen Men. Portrayed as the cream of an already elite regiment, they are such a familiar part of the *Sharpe* films that it comes as something of a surprise to find that they do not exist in the novels, and that their deployment in real life was somewhat different.

'Chosen Man' is the original term for a lance-corporal. Selected from the ranks for their intelligence, they were spared ordinary duties and given command of eight soldiers apiece instead. Some eventually became NCOs.

Instead of sprinkling the Chosen Men throughout the regiment, as they were in real life, screenwriter Eoghan Harries chose to group them around Sharpe, supplying his leading character with a close-knit group of associates – a kind of Dirty half-Dozen – whose dialogue and relationships give the films emotional and comic depth. The technique was so successful that Bernard Cornwell adopted it in the book *Sharpe's Battle*.

• HAGMAN •

Daniel Hagman is the best marksman in the company, and when there's only one chance to make a shot tell, invariably Hagman is called upon to make it.

In this respect John Tams and his character are poles apart. Far from being a crack shot, John is myopic. 'I tend to be careful with the bayonets,' he observes wryly. 'I don't judge distances well.'

But in other ways he and Hagman are very much alike. Both modest, quiet fellows, Hagman hails from Cheshire, and John lives in Derbyshire. Hagman is the oldest of the Chosen Men, and John's the oldest of the actors who play them. Hagman's a poacher, while John is a third-generation settled traveller.

The Chosen Men in action: (Above left) Perkins and Tongue with Sharpe and Harper; (Right) in 'Sharpe's Enemy'

John Tams as Hagman: actor, composer and musician

He is also a musician. A onetime member of the Albion Band, he collects folk music, and reckons that if pressed, he could play 'Abide With Me' on about 30 different instruments. Interestingly, the fiddle – his main musical instrument in *Sharpe* – isn't one of them.

John's involvement with the *Sharpe* films is similarly wide-ranging. As well as starring in them, and reading and commenting on the scripts, he co-writes and performs the scores, writing a new verse for the closing theme, 'Over The Hills And Far Away', for each film. 'Folk songs are very robust,' he says. 'You can change them round a bit, and they'll spring back into shape.'

Although a former music director of the Cottesloe Theatre, and composer of several film scores, John doesn't read music. On *Sharpe* scores, he works with Dominic Muldowney. 'Dominic is the proper classical musician and I'm the illiterate one. He does the orchestrations, and I try to bugger 'em up.'

John stands by the decision – questioned by some – to use electric guitars in the opening titles of the films. 'It's a good instrument to represent a cavalry sword. We have a sizeable audience of young people – I get letters from kids of 10, 12, 14 – and I think the guitar helps to catch their imagination.

Off-screen, John and Sean are good friends. 'I see Sean in Sheffield from time to time. But he's so well-known, it's a bit like going out for a curry with Mother Theresa.'

• HARRIS •

When first introduced to Sharpe, Harris describes himself ironically as 'a courtier to my Lord Bacchus, and an unremitting debtor'. Sharpe correctly translates this as a rake and a wastrel, which Harper subsequently reduces to 'a broken-down scribbler'. It's not a promising start. In fact, Harris is the intellectual of the group. Unusually for a private, he not only reads and writes, but knows literature and speaks several foreign languages. His French comes in handy when Sharpe and the Chosen Men have to bluff their way through enemy lines, he is a dab hand at deciphering French secret codes, and – as we see in *Mission* – knows enough classical poetry to spot a literary fraud when he sees one.

With his flowing red locks, and spare, muscular body, actor Jason Salkey manages to make Harris much more than the company egghead. A former freestyle Frisbee champion, his physical fitness and have-a-go attitude to stunts pay dividends on-screen. Indeed, it's a point of honour for Jason that if a Frenchman needs pulling off his horse, or

Jason Salkey as 'the Rambo intellectual' - Rifleman Harris

WEAPONS

- The rifles used by Sharpe and the Chosen Men are reproductions of the originals and were made by Richard Moore, military adviser on the *Sharpe* films, and members of the Napoleonic Association.

- The Brown Bess musket was the weapon of the British redcoat. Relatively accurate up to 75 yards, it was most effective fired at close range in volleys of 50 to 100 guns. Sharpe insisted that his men fire three rounds a minute, 'whatever the weather' – a reference to the musket's susceptibility to damp – with practice, they could manage four.

- The Baker rifle, though slower to load, came into its own in the hands of a skilled rifleman. Designed by Ezekiel Baker in 1800, it was accurate at 200 yards, and effective up to 400. The Baker rifle revolutionised warfare by enabling a common soldier to kill at long distances: until then, says Richard, the inaccuracy of the musket meant it took a soldier's weight in lead to kill him. The 95th Rifles was the first regiment in an army to be entirely armed with rifles, and the legendary accuracy and range of its men played a significant role in Napoleon's defeat.

- Harper's seven-barrelled volley gun was given to him by Sharpe as a mark of their friendship. Originally designed by Henry Nock in 1798 for naval use, its immense weight and powerful recoil made it unpopular onboard ship where it risked knocking its user over-

Daragh O'Malley with the huge seven-barrelled volley gun made for him for the film 'Sharpe's Company'

board. On land, it took a man as big as Harper to handle it. Richard, who made the gun, says it is the biggest and most powerful muzzle-loading personal weapon in use in film today.

- Sharpe's sword was equally distinctive. Instead of carrying the short curved sabre of the Light Infantry as did his peers, he favoured the massive, straight-bladed 1796 British Heavy Cavalry sword. So heavy that it was virtually impossible to parry, it was used like a bludgeon to smash aside bayonet thrusts and light swords alike.

- The swords used in Sharpe are real weapons, with the exception of that made by Harper in *Sword*, which was made from scratch in Yalta.

- Teresa, the Spanish partisan leader and Sharpe's first wife, earned her reputation as a fighter with a stiletto and a French short sword, but she also carries two naval boarding pistols with spring bayonets. Designed to be used at close range, these were particularly effective when loaded with broken glass, nails, crockery or buckshot.

- Ellie Nugent, the young Irish woman in the film Sharpe's Gold, uses a Pennsylvania rifle with a 44-inch barrel. Its close rifling made it accurate for small game up to 100 yards.

- Despite the weaponry in use, it is estimated that only one in 20 casualties in the British army were the result of battlefield injury. The other 19 were due to disease, poor nutrition or bad surgery.

For Michael Mears, the Rifles are a family tradition

a powder keg needs exploding, he will do it.

Inevitably, he's been hurt. 'I've bashed hips, knees and elbows quite a lot. We all have. One of the worst occasions was in *Honour*, where we free Sharpe from the French. As we left the fort, I set fire to a keg of gunpowder, and there was a bit too much there and my hand got burnt.' Nevertheless, Jason is committed to doing the job properly. 'The audience don't want to see us flinch on screen. They want us to be hard.'

Unlike the others, Harris's character has no first name and doesn't exist in the novels. Jason used a military diary of the period, *The Recollections of Rifleman Harris*, as a source book. The result has been a powerful, engaging character: intelligent without being high-brow, and strong without being stupid. Harris is, as Jason puts it, 'a Rambo intellectual.'

It's very different from the role he was best known for before *Sharpe*: the 'sickeningly clean-living guy' in a Miller Lite commercial.

• COOPER •

Cooper comes from Shoreditch and describes himself as 'a trader in property', By which he means other people's property. He also has an eye for the ladies and a dry sense of humour. Like Hagman, Cooper's criminal past enables him to represent the many thousands of British soldiers who enlisted rather than go to prison for crimes. His best line is in *Rifles* when Sharpe asks for the loan of his picklock. Cooper feigns disbelief: 'Picklock, sir? Catch me with a picklock!' Eventually he consents to lend it, on condition it is returned. 'Trust me', says Sharpe, to which Cooper reasonably responds 'it's very hard to trust a man who wants to borrow your picklock'.

Michael Mears, who plays Cooper, has a particular affinity with the Rifles. His great uncle Thomas ran away to join the Rifles at the start of the Boer War. When he reached South Africa, he sent home a message on a bit of a cigarette packet saying 'This is all I could find to write on. I'm all right and I hope to see you soon'. Michael wrote the same words to his family on his arrival in Yalta almost a hundred years later.

• PERKINS •

In the *Sharpe* films, Lyndon Davis's character Ben Perkins starts out as Major Dunnet's drummer boy and flag carrier. When he and Captain Murray are caught in a French ambush, Sharpe rescues them, and Perkins later returns the favour by shooting dead a French colonel and saving Sharpe's life, thus earning a place among the Chosen Men.

'We had to learn to march, do graveside salutes, and drill until it was second nature. I don't think I could hack the army at all.' Maybe not, but after all that training, he must be a good shot. 'I've won a few cuddly bears in fairgrounds', says Lyndon modestly.

In *Battle*, after three years on the show, Perkins dies. It was an emotional experience.

'I wasn't amazingly happy to be killed. It was very emotional, not just in terms of portraying the death on screen, but also because I then had to go home when everyone else was staying. It wasn't a nice feeling.'

Lyndon Davies as Perkins: 'I don't think I could hack the army'

Paul Trussell as Rifleman Tongue: A bible-thumping soldier who knew no other life but the army

• TONGUE •

Paul Trussell plays the tall, lanky and deeply melancholy Rifleman Tongue in *Rifles* and *Eagles*. He sings hymns loudly and tunelessly, and quotes from the bible in taverns, but he's not above a little wenching when the mood takes him. He has been in the army for as long as he can remember, he doesn't know where he's from and has no family.

• KELLY •

Last of all is Kelly, the posthumous Chosen Man. Morgan Jones plays Kelly, a former Connaught Ranger who joined Hakeswill's deserters in the film *Sharpe's Enemy*. But he's a soldier not a mutineer, and when Sharpe wages war on the deserters, Kelly is relieved to be invited to join. After a brave fight he is fatally wounded; as he dies Sharpe presses the coveted stripe into Kelly's hand, making him a Chosen Man.

SOLDIERING

The basic unit of the army in 1809, the battalion, contained between 600 and 1000 men. Most regiments had two battalions, each containing ten companies. Of these, the crack companies were the Light and the Grenadiers.

The red tunics, white cross-belts and black shakoes of the British infantry were designed to exaggerate size and strength, giving them a psychological advantage over the enemy. Regimental jackets were differentiated by the colour of collars and cuffs - yellow, in the case of the South Essex - the style of the lace, and the design of the buttons.

Soldiers were paid one shilling and one penny a day. After deductions for rations, washing, pipeclay and blackball, boot repairs and subs to the military hospitals, and stoppages for items lost or stolen, privates could expect the princely sum of about fourpence halfpenny a day in return for risking their lives for their country.

Although not averse to enforcing discipline with the lash, Wellington knew the value of keeping his men fed, paid and given their drink ration. As a result, his army - like almost no others - could be relied upon to stand and fight.

The elite rifle regiments dressed and fought differently from the redcoats. As skirmishing and reconnaissance units, they were trusted to work alone and use their own initiative, and were traditionally excused the menial duties of soldiering such as ditch-digging. The Riflemen prided themselves on being first into the field, and last out of it, and their special responsibilities were denoted by their dark green jackets.

Sharpe's Allies:
Wellington, Hogan, Nairn, Munro and Ross

Wellington has been played by two actors – David Troughton in the first year, and Hugh Fraser thereafter – and in both cases, every appearance was preceded by at least two hours in make-up to affix the huge and imperious prosthetic nose that was his distinguishing feature.

David Troughton, well-known as Dr Bob Buzzard in *A Very Peculiar Practice*, plays Wellington – then merely Sir Arthur Wellesley – in the crucial opening scene in which Sharpe rescues him from some French cavalry. David had to ride hell for leather across a stream, but his Russian-speaking stunt horse interpreted his sign for 'halt' as a command to rear. Troughton found himself in the river – having neatly repeated the move his stunt double had just done for him.

In subsequent years, the role has been played by Hugh Fraser.

One key respect in which author Bernard Cornwell admits having taken liberties with historical accuracy is in the organisation surrounding Wellington. In order to allow Sharpe and Wellington to interact directly, Bernard reduced what was probably a five-tier chain of command between Wellington and Sharpe to a single intelligence officer.

• HOGAN AND NAIRN •

Wellington's head of intelligence has been played by four different actors to date. Although all four have shared certain common features, each has made the character his own.

The spymaster in the first two films is Major Hogan, played by Brian Cox. Short, plump, middle-aged, and snuff-taking, he is nominally an engineer, but as Wellington says in *Eagle*, Hogan's coat buttons up tight over a number of other duties. His official duties are to reconnoitre routes for the army, reporting on which roads are passable, where key bridges lie and whether they will bear the weight of heavy artillery. Unofficially, he is Wellington's contact with a network of spies within British ranks and among the Spanish partisans.

A well-known classical actor and author, Brian has done a great deal of screen acting, taking roles in the Channel 4 drama *The Big Battalions*, the BBC's *Grushko* and *The Cloning of Joanna May*, and playing Hannibal Lecter in the film *Manhunter*.

(Below) Brian Cox as Major Hogan

(Right) The Duke of Wellington led the British to victory in the Peninsular War

Michael Byrne as the crusty Nairn,
Wellington's second head of intelligence

Dundee-born Brian is often cast as a Scot – he has subsequently appeared in the feature films *Braveheart* and *Rob Roy* – but in *Sharpe*, he plays an Irishman, beneath whose disarmingly genial exterior is a razor-sharp mind and a courageous heart. Although Sharpe knows Hogan won't always tell him everything, he trusts the man's integrity and courage and the two men are friends.

Hogan was replaced for the next three films by Major Nairn. The actor Michael Byrne played Nairn as a very different character – grave, serious, and every inch Wellington's right-hand man. Unlike Hogan, he was not an easy man for Sharpe to like, and in *Company*, there are strong undertones of his disapproval of Sharpe's headstrong ways.

• MUNRO AND ROSS •

In the third year, Wellington's head of intelligence was the irascible Scot, Major Mungo Munro, played by Hugh Ross. Says casting director John Hubbard, 'We needed to differentiate Munro somehow from Hogan and Nairn, so we made him more flamboyant, more humorous. There were lots of hats, lots of tartan, and, of course, a passion for the pipes.'

Hugh's successor is James Laurenson, who plays Major General Ross in the fourth and fifth years of *Sharpe*. Ross is not just Sharpe's immediate boss, but also his friend – as we see when he gives the bride away at Sharpe's wedding. James, who has worked extensively in the US, recently appeared in *Prime Suspect* and has twice been in *Taggart*.

As John Hubbard explains, Hogan, Nairn, Munro and Ross fulfil the same function not simply as Wellington's head of intelligence, but in adding another dimension to the story: 'They're all rather cheeky, naughty characters,' says John. 'They don't always tell Sharpe – and therefore the audience – the whole story. It's always fun casting them: all the work is in the sly glance, the innuendo, and the asides to Wellington when Sharpe leaves the room.'

James Laurenson as Maj. Gen. Ross, the
intelligence chief in 'Regiment', 'Siege',
'Mission' and 'Revenge'

Sharpe's Adversaries:
Ducos, Brand, Hakeswill, and Simmerson

S harpe's principal antagonist is, of course, Napoleon, but apart from a brief glimpse in *Sharpe's Waterloo*, the two never come face to face. Instead, it is Napoleon's leading spies, commanders and double agents whom Sharpe confronts.

• DUCOS •

In *Enemy*, the tactical military antagonist is Pierre Ducos, Napoleon's chief spymaster. A cold and sinister figure, his lack of compassion – particularly for women – is matched only by his dislike of Sharpe. In the film *Sharpe's Honour*, Ducos gives Napoleon an undertaking to get the British out of Spain by striking a deal with collaborators among the Spanish nobility. His price is the death of Sharpe, but his plans are foiled by the arrival of the Chosen Men, and it is Ducos himself who gets shot – ironically, by one of his own soldiers.

Ducos's return in the film *Sharpe's Siege* will come as a surprise to those viewers who remember him sitting in stiff-legged, open-eyed rictus with a French bullet in his back. But, says actor Feodor Atkine who plays Ducos, this scene was deliberately ambiguous and was used in preference to another – also shot – in which Sharpe stands over Ducos's body, verifying his death.

Major Ducos (Feodor Atkine), Napoleon's chief spy - and Sharpe's deadly enemy

Mark Strong as the arrogant Brand

According to Feodor, his character is the embodiment of Fouché, a leading statesman under four successive French regimes – royalist and republican – of the period. Cunning, duplicitous and utterly without moral scruples.

Athough a formidable adversary, Ducos is not a courageous figure, and he rarely confronts Sharpe on equal terms. The interrogation scene in *Honour* is a case in point: Ducos is fierce enough while his opponent is bound, but when Sharpe frees himself, he flees.

Nevertheless, Feodor manages to imbue his character with a quiet menace, using skills learnt when he studied with the virtuoso Parisian mime, Etienne Decroux, and the Japanese kabuki master, Sensei Onoe.

Not all Sharpe's antagonists are so obviously aligned. In *Honour*, the Spanish inquisitor Father Hacha (Nickolas Grace) and his brother, the partisan known as El Matarife (Matthew Scurfield) – supposedly allies of the British – turn out to be in the pay of Ducos.

• BRAND •

Similarly, in *Siege*, Maquerre, played by Christian Brendel, poses as a French collaborator but turns out to be a double agent, and in

Oscar-nominee Pete Postlethwaite as the evil Sgt. Hakeswill, Sharpe's infamous adversary

Mission, the French protagonist is actually an English aristocrat, Colonel Brand, whose reputation for daring and valour is a carefully constructed front for his activities on behalf of the French. Brand is played by Mark Strong.

By comparison, Sharpe's other French adversaries are refreshingly honest about their allegiances. Pot Au Feu, for example, the fiery French marshal who leads the mutineers in *Enemy*, and Cresson, a French officer in *Siege*, may be ruthless rogues, but at least you know which side they're on. Calvet, however, is more complex. In *Siege* and *Mission*, he is Sharpe's

enemy, but in *Revenge*, during the Bourbons' brief return, he and Sharpe join forces to defeat the duplicitous Ducos.

• HAKESWILL •

Some of Sharpe's most memorable antagonists, however, are from his own side. Undoubtedly the most celebrated is Sgt. Obadiah Hakeswill, played by Pete Postlethwaite, whose cruel eyes and nervous twitch all but upstaged Sean Bean in the second year of *Sharpe*.

Hakeswill is a liar, a thief and a bully. The

enmity between him and Sharpe goes back to their days in India where Sharpe had once prevented Hakeswill from torturing a man to death. The wily sergeant had countered by passing the abuse off as his accuser's and as a result, Sharpe was flogged.

Born in Warrington, Shropshire, Pete was 48 when he played Hakeswill – though he refers to him affectionately as 'Obadiah' – and his shaven head and blackened teeth were so good that his five-year-old son Will failed to recognise him.

In his Oscar-nominated performance as Giuseppe Conlon in *In The Name Of The Father*, Pete modelled his character on his own late father. Obadiah Hakeswill, however, wasn't modelled on anyone. 'He didn't need to be', says Pete. 'You just open Bernard Cornwell's novels and he walks off the page.'

Pete's strongest memory of filming *Sharpe* is at the scene of his own execution: 'I remember the look on Sean's face when we did the cutaways. There was more than satisfaction in his eyes at the sight of his enemy dying: there was a sadness there too, a sense of loss. In one way, he's actually sad to see Obadiah go.'

And that's the whole point, says Pete: Sharpe and Obadiah are two sides of the same coin. They're from similar backgrounds, they both dragged themselves up from the gutter, but while Sharpe fights for justice and law, Hakeswill robs, rapes and murders.

In Pete's view, it was his long-standing friendship with Sean – dating back to the days they were in the RSC together – which enabled them both to convey such mutual hatred. 'It was only because we knew and loved each other that we had enough trust to be so horrible to each other.'

For an actor so well known for playing villains – the bullying father in *Distant Voices, Still Lives*, Montague Tig in the BBC's *Martin Chuzzlewit*, and the sinister Mr. Kobayashi in *The Usual Suspects*, to name but a few – Pete has avoided being typecast by giving moving performances of a gentler kind. He plays the trainer, Ken, in *When Saturday Comes* (also starring Sean), Mitch in the BBC's *Sin Bin*, and of course, Giuseppe.

Of all the characters Pete's played in his career, which is the one that people remember when he gets stopped in the street? 'Obadiah,' he says. 'No question.' And after that? 'Someone did ask me the other day about that film I was in called How's Your Father?...'

• SIMMERSON •

The most resilient of Sharpe's enemies, and the only British one to appear in three different years, is the British colonel, Sir Henry Simmerson.

Simmerson arrives in Spain in 1809, as colonel of the South Essex. So rich is he – and so desperate for glory – that he has bought not only his commission, but his regiment too. Obsessed by rules and regulations, he insists his men adhere to military textbooks in every regard. When they don't, he flogs them indiscriminately – an activity from which he gains a peculiar sadistic pleasure.

By repeatedly standing up for justice in the face of cruelty and cowardice, Sharpe quickly makes an enemy of Simmerson. Their hostility continues long after the battle at Valdelacasa in which Sir Henry loses the King's Colours. It survives their encounter at Villafranca in 1812, and comes to a head in London in 1813, when Sharpe exposes Simmerson's involvement in the scandal of the missing regiment.

The genial personality and ribald sense of humour of actor Michael Cochrane contrast sharply with the barbarism of the character he plays, and on set Simmerson's trademark 'hurumph' – pepperish when annoyed, indignant when cornered – invariably sparks gales of laughter among cast and crew.

In the new films, Sharpe repeatedly confronts Rossendale, his wife's lover. But Rossendale is no fighter, and for Sharpe, the real threat comes from Ducos and several men who are – nominally, at least – on his own side, such as Wickham, Parfitt and the Prince of Orange.

The barbaric Col. Sir Henry Simmerson - played by the genial Michael Cochrane

Sharpe's Companions

ach battalion was allowed sixty soldiers' wives overseas, but a gaggle of other women joined the troop, selling themselves as seamstresses, washerwomen and prostitutes. One of these was Ramona, Harper's lover, later to become his wife.

• TERESA •

The women to whom Sharpe was drawn were of a different kind. Comandante Teresa, the Spanish aristocrat turned partisan leader, had seen her family murdered by the French. She herself was raped, and as a result, she is fiercely determined to drive the French out of her country. She joined the partisans, and her notable skill with a sword earned her the title 'La Aguja' or 'The Needle'.

Teresa is played by the Spanish actress Assumpta Serna, who based her portrayal on records of a real Spanish heroine of the period, Agustina of Aragon. Agustina fought at the sieges of Zaragoza and Tortosa, and in the front

Teresa's fighting skills earnt Sharpe's respect, and her compassion earned his love

Assumpta Serna as Comandante Teresa

line at Vitoria. Twice captured by the French – she escaped both times – she was appointed an officer of the Spanish army and was received in Cadiz by Wellington. 'She was a kind of Joan of Arc figure,' says Assumpta. 'She came from a very rich family in Aragon, and although she didn't hide the fact that she was female, she dressed as a man when she went into battle.' Unlike Teresa, Agustina survived the war and died peacefully in Andalucia.

'Agustina was said to be a woman with no mercy, but who knows what suffering – physically and intellectually – she had been

through?' says Assumpta. 'In the first two episodes, I tried to be that kind of closed person. Teresa doesn't enjoy what she does: she fights because she must. She is very single-minded about it until she meets Sharpe.'

In the film *Sharpe's Company*, says Assumpta, Teresa changes a little. 'She became a women more than a fighter,' adding in her beautiful and slightly flawed English, 'She has a little girl, and she was a little bit retired.'

But even though she was at home, she was still planning the resistance. 'That's why she never looks really comfortable in a dress,' says

Assumpta. 'For more than six years, she had worn men's clothes. But she's able to use dresses as a disguise. She wears a dress to catch two sentinels off their guard before she stabs them, and again with the French officer that she kills. Women do that today, too. We wear dresses to be more effective with business men, to obtain what we want.'

There are parallels between actress and character. As a young student in Spain, Assumpta was active against Franco. She joined a radical theatre company and took part in marches and demonstrations.

Years later, while she played a Spanish guerrilla leader in the remote hills of the Ukraine, she would remember those days. 'One time, I had to go into a village after a massacre. It reminded me of going into the law faculty against 'The Grey Ones' (Spanish slang for the police). You get something from everyone.'

Well-known for her roles as murderous or manipulative women in *Matador*, *Wild Orchid*, *The Fencing Master* and *Falcon Crest*, Assumpta enjoyed playing a heroine for once. But she acknowledges that there were limitations to the role: 'I knew that this is a series for men, it is an exaltation of manhood. It's not necessarily macho, but the values are very male. Men were very protected on camera, and I knew I couldn't expect a nice lens pointing at me, or real character development because I was there for love interest.'

Had it been up to her, she says, she might have done it differently – particularly the scene in which she is killed by the evil Hakeswill, who shoots her in cold blood in *Sharpe's Enemy*: 'For me, it wasn't built up enough and the scene where I'm killed was too quick. I discussed it with Tom, but I didn't win.'

Teresa dies with Sharpe at her side, in a tender and moving scene. Off camera, however, her tenderness was reserved for Scott

The brave Teresa dies in Sharpe's arms

Cleverdon, who plays Harry Price, the goodhearted lieutenant in the film *Sharpe's Company* who is always borrowing money and who has to drink to get up enough courage to go into battle. Assumpta and Scott got married some months later.

• LADY FARTHINGDALE •

Although largely faithful to Teresa during their marriage, Sharpe has one brief interlude with Lady Isabella Farthingdale. Played by Elizabeth Hurley, Lady Farthingdale is a former prostitute who managed to catch an aristocratic husband.

Many years before, Sharpe had been a client of Isabella's, and they meet again when she is held to ransom by the odious Hakeswill in *Enemy*. Refreshingly modern in her attitude to marriage and sex, she makes no secret of the fact that she still fancies Sharpe.

According to casting director John Hubbard, Liz Hurley was perfect for the role. 'I like Elizabeth enormously. I'd seen her in a lot of things over the past couple of years. I wanted a lady who was posh and a bit fiery. Spirited and quite sexy. And there's not a big list of people in that area. I approached her quite early on, but I didn't think we'd get her.'

Liz had appeared in another Picture Palace serial, Channel 4's *The Orchid House*, but her biggest roles – on and off the screen – were still before her.

'We do deliberately try to get people who are going to be very well known in a year's time,' continues John. 'It's good to have people who are going up for lots of movies. As it happened, that turned out to be the year that Liz wore 'That Dress', and that Pete Postlethwaite got nominated for the Oscar. You can't buy that sort of publicity.'

THE SPANIARDS

As Bernard Cornwell notes at the end of *Rifles*, the bravura style of Wellington's victories in Spain often obscures the fact that the Spanish people killed more French soldiers than the British ever managed to. Although the Spanish armies did not enjoy great success in the field after 1808, civilian partisans caused a great deal of damage to the occupying French under cover of night by assassination, poisoning and theft. At their height, these actions – collectively known as the *guerrilla*, or 'the little war' – cost Napoleon 400 casualties a day and stretched manpower to the limit in extra guard duties. In addition, Wellington paid in gold for captured French messages, and it is said that if Napoleon wanted to be certain of getting a letter safely across Spain in 1810, it took 1200 soldiers to do it.

Some Spanish sided with the French; they were known as 'afrancesados'.

Elizabeth Hurley as Isabella in 'Enemy'

• LA MARQUESA •

After the death of Teresa, Sharpe goes into a deep and prolonged depression, and the woman who does most to reawaken his emotional side is La Marquesa.

The feisty Marquesa – who works for Napoleon, and is used by Ducos to foment trouble between Wellington and his Spanish allies – is played by Alice Krige, then fresh from the BBC's adaptation of Stendhal's *Scarlet And Black*.

Alice was given elaborately curled hair for the part, which was quite a departure from her normally straight blond locks. Even though she spent a lot of time in curlers – even going out in them – the curls dropped a little in the cold

and required the work of four hairdressers to stay in shape.

One particularly cold day, while filming a scene in which she and Sean are escaping on horseback, Alice gave the hairdressers an even greater headache. On their fourth take of a shot in which their horse gallops across a ford, she and Sean fell off into an ice-cold river. The hairdressers weren't the only ones to gasp in horror. But director Tom Clegg saw that the fall added drama, and quickly re-wrote the scene to include it.

• ELLIE NUGENT and LADY KIELY •

Though Sharpe and La Marquesa seem to hit it off, she returns to Paris, and on his next adventure, Sharpe is attracted to a spirited young Irish woman named Ellie Nugent.

Played by Jayne Ashbourne, Ellie is in Spain to seek her father, who has disappeared. Although less worldly than La Marquesa, she is no less bold. Ellie can handle a gun, says Jayne, and when she wants something, she goes for it.

In *Gold*, Ellie's goal is to find her father, and to explore her emerging attraction to Sharpe along the way. She does both.

The enigmatic Lady Kiely is the love interest in *Battle*. Although a beautiful and

intelligent woman, she is one of the few Sharpe doesn't in fact bed. This isn't for want of the opportunity. Desperate to win back her philandering husband, Lady Kiely – played by Allie Byrne – asks Sharpe for his help, offering her body in return.

• LASS and LADY ANNE CAMOYNES •

Allie Byrne as Lady Kiely in 'Battle'

With characteristic gallantry, Sharpe declines. In *Sword*, he is not so principled. This time the lover is Lass (Emily Mortimer), a young novice nun so traumatised by her experiences in the war that she becomes mute. Somewhat quixotically perhaps, sex with Sharpe restores her

Alice Krige as the Marquesa in 'Honour'

Emily Mortimer as Lass in 'Sword'

Jayne Ashbourne as Ellie in 'Gold'

powers of speech.

The first woman to bed Sharpe – as opposed to the other way round – is the aristocratic Lady Anne Camoynes in *Regiment*. Lady Anne, played by Caroline Langrishe, is the reluctant mistress of Lord Fenner, and she switches allegiance when she realises that Sharpe can help her ruin the man she hates.

Caroline Langrishe as Lady Anne

• JANE GIBBONS •

If Lady Anne – familiar from the BBC's *Lovejoy* – is setting her highly fashionable hat at Sharpe, she is pipped to the post by Jane Gibbons, whom Sharpe falls in love with and later marries.

At first sight, Jane is not half the woman Lady Anne is. Nor is she up to the standards set by her predecessor, the fiery Teresa. She is sheltered, provincial, and very unworldly, and at first it's difficult to imagine why Sharpe falls for her.

But beneath Jane's soft exterior lies a certain steel. She knows what poverty and suffering are: the orphaned daughter of a saddler, she has been brought up by her uncle, the odious Sir Henry Simmerson, who beats her and plans to marry her off to one of his cronies, Lt. Col. Girdwood. So when Jane agrees to help Sharpe uncover her uncle's shady practices,

she is exhibiting immense personal courage.

Sharpe, for his own part, had fallen for her when he'd seen a miniature of her years before. Cherishing this paragon of beauty in his heart, when he finally meets her, he puts his life in her hands. She in turn is drawn to his sense of honour and thirst for justice.

Abigail Cruttenden, who plays Jane Gibbons, denies her character is wet.

'Women were treated very differently in those days. Even if you were educated, your interests had to be limited to poetry and painting. Jane lived an incredibly isolated existence. Although she's scared a lot of the time, she has good reason to be. She knows that given half a chance, Simmerson will beat her.'

Small wonder, then, that Jane is attracted to Sharpe. 'She herself has a strong sense of right and wrong, and when she discovers what's happening to the soldiers, she allies herself not with her uncle, but with the men,' says Abigail. 'She dares to run away, and dares to steal food and money for Sharpe.'

Jane's courage shows later too. 'In *Siege*, she insists on visiting Major General Ross when he's got fever, despite the danger, and later, after her own illness, she makes herself useful by becoming a nurse.' She also sleeps with Sharpe before they are married, which is fairly modern.

But it is in *Mission* that she seems to get things wrong. Being an army wife is not enough for her, and while Sharpe is away, she flirts wildly with the poet Shellington, blind to the fact that he's a cad and a charlatan. Still, Abigail defends her:

'Until then, Jane's not been particularly interested in society,' she says. 'But after a while, she discovers that Sharpe isn't married to her so much as to the army. He's away a lot, and she's often alone – nearly as isolated as she was before she married. Life in barracks must have been pretty dull for most women, but especially

Abigail Cruttenden as Jane Gibbons

hard for Jane, whose husband is looked down upon by his fellow officers, and worshipped by his men, so she's got no-one to talk to. For Jane, flirting is a way to get close to people. Jane Austen's novels are about this. Women's lives were very constrained, and for some of her characters, flirting is a way of expressing something other than perfect strait-jacketed modesty.'

The marriage ends when Jane has an affair. Sharpe is recovering from gunshot wounds in France at the time, and is trying to resist his own attraction to Lucille, the young French widow who nurses him back to health. When he learns of Jane's affair, however, he lets things with Lucille take their natural course.

As we know, though, Sharpe is no saint where women are concerned. He allows himself a second brief fling with Lady Anne in *Sharpe's Justice* before going home to Lucille in *Waterloo*.

Opening Salvoes

Set in Spain, shot in the Ukraine, and calling for a cast of thousands, 'Sharpe' was widely thought too ambitious for British television. Here's how the sceptics were proved wrong.

Getting Started

British re-enactors led by Sharpe's historical advisor, Richard Moore (far right), played Redcoats in 'Sharpe's Regiment'

Muir Sutherland first read *Sharpe's Eagle* in 1986 at the suggestion of Andy Allan, director of programmes at Central Television. Andy had worked with Bernard Cornwell on Thames News, and was keen that Central should be the broadcaster for a prestige production of this type.

Muir – also a former member of Thames Television, where he had been director of programmes – agreed that *Sharpe* would make great television. He took an option not only on *Eagle*, but on all subsequent Sharpe books.

Central's head of drama Ted Childs had an abiding interest in military history and was equally sure *Sharpe* would make exciting television. But could it be done on television budgets? And – equally importantly – would it look authentic?

The challenge was always the sheer scale of the battles. The books often called for regiments of 600 soldiers and 40 officers, and for full-scale battles between 40,000 soldiers. How does one reduce that to a size that television can afford without it looking hopelessly thin and unexciting?

Muir acknowledged that the films would not be cheap. Top quality television drama costs around £600,000 per hour, and it was clear that these films were going to be more expensive than that. However, he argued that by focusing on Sharpe's activities behind enemy lines rather than the large-scale battles, and by attracting production partners who could bring their own money, he could keep costs to a manageable level. And as the books demonstrated, these films would have a strong appeal for the audience which television finds the hardest to reach: upmarket men. Central agreed to give it a try.

BERNARD CORNWELL – NOVELIST

The *Sharpe* books are adventure stories,' says their creator, Bernard Cornwell. 'They're about a world where you can kick the boss in the teeth and get the girl. They're not intended to be great literature.'

That doesn't stop them being meticulously researched – with the exception of *Siege* and *Enemy*, all the books are based on real events.

Bernard admires the films enormously and has no quarrel with their adaptation:

'If I'm in trouble with the plot, I can wheel on 50,000 French and slaughter a few of 'em,' he observes. 'You can't do that on television because it costs too much. That's why the films are much more character-driven than the books, and that's why Eoghan invented the Chosen Men. I put them into the book *Sharpe's Battle*, but they were Eoghan's idea.'

He also finds the image of Sean eclipses the earlier vision he had of Sharpe as a dark-haired Cockney. 'Sean wiped the original Sharpe from my mind, and I think he's terrific.'

Born in South Essex in 1944, Bernard was adopted at the age of six weeks by two members of a strict fundamentalist sect called the Peculiar People. Bernard grew up in a household that forbade alcohol, cigarettes, dances, television, conventional medicine and toy guns. Not surprisingly, he developed a fascination for military adventures. As a teenager, he devoured CS Forester's *Hornblower* novels and tried to enlist three times.

Poor eyesight put paid to his dream, instead Bernard went to university to read theology. On graduating, he became a teacher, then joined BBC's *Nationwide*, working his way up the ladder to become head of current affairs at BBC Northern Ireland, then editor of *Thames News*. Then in 1979, his life changed. He fell in love with an American.

'Judy couldn't live here, so I gave up my job and moved to the US. I couldn't get a green card, and for 18 months, the only thing I could do was write novels.' The result was *Sharpe's Eagle*.

The first agent he sent it to returned it saying British readers aren't interested in stories about the army. Eventually Heinemann's offered him £3,000 for world rights. 'I jumped up and down for several minutes,' says Bernard. 'Then it dawned on me that £3,000 wasn't enough to keep me alive long enough to write a second book.'

That same evening, he met an English literary agent at a thanksgiving party. 'I told him I'd just written a novel. Of course he turned round and walked off, but I followed, clutching my bloody

Bernard Cornwell: 'Anyone who behaved the way Sharpe did would have been out of the army in three months'

Mary, and said "I already have an offer". "How much?" I told him. "Well it must be a bloody awful book then," and he walked off again.' Undeterred, Bernard took the manuscript to the agent's office the next day. 'That night he phoned me and said 'How much do you want?' Bernard eventually got $100,000 for the first three *Sharpe* books. A seven-book deal in the UK soon followed.

Bernard started working eight hours a day, averaging two books a year. By the time British TV caught on, there were six *Sharpe* books in print. Now there are thirteen, and collectively they've sold over 2 million copies around the world.

Sharpe has enabled Bernard to buy houses in Cape Cod and Florida, and two boats. He takes two months off a year, much of which he spends on his 24 foot Cornish crabber *Royalist*.

It's a life Bernard heartily enjoys – for all that Eoghan Harris gently mocks him: 'Take my advice,' Eoghan has Sharpe say to Rifleman Harris in *Sharpe's Sword*. 'When you get back home, write a bloody good book with loads of shooting in it, and you'll die a rich man.'

'That's just Eoghan's little joke,' says Bernard. Then he laughs. 'I got my own back in my script notes.'

creenwriter Eoghan Harris was commissioned to write scripts adapted from the first two books – *Sharpe's Eagle* and *Sharpe's Gold* – together with one from a new book, *Sharpe's Rifles*, which Bernard Cornwell hastily story-lined to set the stage for the entire endeavour.

In 1988, Muir hired Kenny McBain, producer of *Inspector Morse* and *Boon*, to get the show started. They did a recce in Spain, visiting all the places where the actual battles took place, and putting together a budget.

Award-winning costume designer John Mollo, whose credits include *Gandhi*, *The Jewel In The Crown*, *Alien* and *Star Wars*, was asked to prepare a list of costume requirements and a budget.

John's brother Andrew, a leading production designer, was already drawing up plans for sets.

Muir set about getting a cash injection from Spanish television which lightened the load by £500,000. Then he went back to Central with the package.

But the budget was still too high, and in 1988 Central put the project on hold. Then, sadly, Kenny died of cancer, and all hopes of making *Sharpe* died with him.

Not quite all. Two years later, the world was changing. The Iron Curtain was coming down and rumours were circulating that filming was cheap behind it. Muir set out to find a new producer prepared to re-examine the prospects of making *Sharpe* – this time, in the unknown environment of Eastern Europe.

More than one turned him down. The television business was risky enough already without making what were effectively feature films on television budgets somewhere where you couldn't even guarantee an electricity supply.

But Muir persisted – where *Sharpe* is concerned, he doesn't understand the meaning of the word 'can't' – and eventually he persuaded Malcolm Craddock to come onboard as a partner. Malcolm was an inspired choice. An award-winning commercials director with several major Channel 4 series to his credit, including *Tandoori Nights*, *Eurocops* and *Four Minutes*, he had a broad range of production experience. His acclaimed serial *The Orchid House*, shot in the Caribbean, demonstrated that he knew a thing or two about making period films in faraway locations.

SCREENWRITERS

hen first approached to adapt Bernard Cornwell's novels for television, says screenwriter Eoghan Harris, it felt as if all his birthdays had come at once. Not only was he an immense fan of the *Sharpe* books as an adult, but he had spent his boyhood immersed in the Victorian action-adventure novels of G.A. Henty and R.M. Ballantyne.

'While other boys were reading *Wizard* and *Rover*, I was engrossed in huge leather-bound volumes of the *Boy's Own Paper*, 1890 to 1900,' says Eoghan. 'Mentally, I spent my childhood on the North West Frontier.'

For an Irishman, Eoghan has unusually close links with the British military. Not only was he in the Territorial Army, but he grew up in Cork, near the Victoria Barracks from which the Duke of Wellington – an Irishman himself – set sail for the Peninsular Wars. Eoghan has regarded Wellington as a personal hero ever since, and he has a fund of stories, not just about the Iron Duke's legendary military victories, but also about his sardonic wit.

Eoghan claims that being Irish freed him to write about honour and courage in the British army in a way that English writers couldn't. 'Left liberalism was all over the British film industry at that time,' he says. 'Having somebody stand in front of the Union Jack and shout "Stand!, Stand!, Stand!" would make most English-born writers deeply uneasy. I was the perfect man for the job because I have no such hang-ups. Being Irish I could wave the union jack and be proud of honour and courage, without feeling I had to defend myself at a Hampstead dinner party.'

It was the fierce belief in the honour code which governed soldiers' behaviour that Eoghan felt he had to put on the screen.

'War was fought under restraints,' he says. 'Men behave appallingly during wars, but they also behave with great gallantry and decency. I had to make clear that such values existed.'

Yet in *Sharpe's Eagle*, Sharpe and Harper kill Lt. Berry in cold blood. How does Eoghan square that with the honour code?

'Sharpe likes law when he can get it, but he believes in justice,' says Eoghan. 'When he's on the field he believes in law, but when he's dealing with someone like Berry, then he will step outside the law to

Screenwriter Eoghan Harris: 'Sharpe is a kind of morality play. There is law, but if it fails you, Sharpe will get you justice'

get justice. *Sharpe* is a kind of morality play. It says that law and justice aren't the same thing. There is law, but if it fails you, Sharpe will get you justice.'

Eoghan brought a screenwriter's critical eye to the adaptation of the novels: 'The *Sharpe* books were wonderful, but I did make two crucial additions. I invented the Chosen Men to make the army intelligible for the small screen, and I added a comic dimension.

'Everyone has their pet theories about why *Sharpe* works, but to me the sense of family is critical. Writing these screenplays in Thatcher's Britain, I was very conscious of the fact that people didn't feel loved or respected. In Sharpe's world, if you play by the rules, the army will give you the utmost respect.'

The relationships between men in this world are often moving. 'As a writer, I'm much more interested in relationships between men than between men and women. I like the emotional life that goes on between men in the army. I'm always looking for that dimension in *Sharpe*.'

When it comes to women, however, Eoghan has a more simplistic view. Some people regard the women in his scripts as at best marginalised, and at worst merely sex objects. So, is Sharpe merely shagging his way through the Peninsular War?

'Sharpe is married to his regiment,' he says. 'His emotional life is with the regiment, not with the women, and he's committing adultery every time he turns to them.'

In Sharpe's world, there are more important things in life than relationships with women. 'This is the classical view of what a man's role is,' says Eoghan. 'It's not a fashionable view, and I make no apologies for that. For many of us it might be more important for a man for to give up his life for his beliefs or his country, rather than putting his family first. The most important thing to me is that Sharpe is a moral human being who behaves well.'

Eoghan has written no less than six of the eleven *Sharpe* films. A confirmed John Ford fan, he sees the films as in the same genre as westerns: tales of revenge and retribution in which the hero's actions are informed by a code of honour and high principles. Eoghan writes scripts with this in mind – adding sexual tension and comic relief when possible.

He is fortunate to have material as rich as the *Sharpe* novels from which to work. Bernard's stories have a number of constant themes which lend themselves well to epic action-adventure films. He always presents his hero with a military goal such as capturing an enemy spy, a personal goal such as winning honour or glory, and the threat of dire consequences – which might take the form of court martial, loss of rank or simply death – if he fails. In addition to his enemies among the ranks of the French, Sharpe faces formidable adversaries on his own side, such as Obadiah Hakeswill, Sir Henry Simmerson and Colonel Brand. And very often he also has a romantic or emotional journey to make in relation to a woman.

The screenwriters faithfully reproduce these elements of the novels on the screen, although each finds their own way to represent the wealth of historical detail which Bernard includes in the novels.

Among the other writers who have contributed to the *Sharpe* opus are veteran screenwriter Charles Wood and rising star Russell Lewis.

Charles, who wrote *Sharpe's Company*, is the author of numerous films, television dramas and plays, including Tony Richardson's film *The Charge of the Light Brigade*, *Tumbledown* and *The Englishman Who Went Up A Hill But Came Down a Mountain*. An enormously experienced writer with a deep knowledge of military history, he underpins the rousing action-adventure of *Sharpe's Company* with subtle characterisation, period dialogue and a distinctly dry sense of humour.

Responsibility for selecting writers and developing scripts is mainly the producers', with some input from the broadcaster, first Central, now Carlton. Malcolm involves himself at every stage, reading the novels, treatments and each draft of the script, and working closely with writer and script editor to get story, characters and dialogue exactly right.

This is not just a creative process, but a practical one. Bernard's novels regularly call for a cast of thousands, and it takes skill and experience to interpret them within the financial and practical constraints of television while still maintaining the feeling of the 'big screen'.

'Malcolm's a very experienced producer and has been a personal friend for more than 20 years,' says Muir. 'He has great strengths at the script stage, as well as a detailed knowledge of production. He's also tremendously tenacious. I knew that if anyone could do it, Malcolm and I could.'

Sharpe was on the road again.

That road took Muir and Malcolm to Slovenia, the Czech Republic and Montenegro in the former Yugoslavia, in search of places that could offer the right combination of locations, personnel and price. Each time, like Goldilocks in the house of the Three Bears, they found something not quite to their liking. The Czech Republic was too expensive, the right team didn't exist in Slovenia, and the former Yugoslavia was already showing signs of unrest. Again, the prospects for *Sharpe* were looking dim.

But they never gave up hope.

'I always believed it was possible to make *Sharpe*,' says Malcolm. 'The only question was whether it could be done for the money. But I remember sitting in a minibus, going down a mountain track in Yugoslavia, and suddenly finding the wheels spinning over a precipitous 2000-foot drop, and thinking "Why on earth am I here?". Fortunately, it wasn't all that bad.'

Back in England, Malcolm and Muir were persuaded by Richard Creasey, Central's dynamic head of features, to consider the Soviet Union. A veteran of more than 70 trips to the former USSR, Richard knew more than anyone else in Britain the potential of a place that was a complete mystery to Western programme makers.

'Forget about what you've heard,' he told Malcolm and Muir. 'Go out there and see for yourselves.'

They did. A recce was arranged in Moscow so that Muir and Malcolm could meet members of the Anglo-Soviet Creative Association, which had been established to further cultural links between Britain and the Soviet Union under the Communist regime. Jointly owned by Central Television and several Russian companies, the Association was staffed by a group of Russians led by Stepan Pojenian, all of whom were resourceful, energetic and keen to show what they could do.

'Stepan looked after the finances, recruiting and contracts of the Russian crew,' says Malcolm. 'He's an ex-boxer and a very determined man.' His colleague Igor Nossov was a top-flight fixer: 'He's one of the few people who can open doors to the top brass in the Crimea, and he's very good at having saunas with the Ukrainain minister of defence, which proved to be essential.'

Muir Sutherland, executive producer (left), and Malcolm Craddock, producer, confer on the set of 'Sharpe's Regiment'

This provided reassurance a few weeks later when there was a coup against Gorbachev. If there was such a thing as a safe pair of hands in the former Soviet Union at that time, Muir and Malcolm knew that they were in them!

Pavel Douvidson, or 'Pasha', handled the day-to-day running of the Russian team. He and his associate Tatyana Shakhgeldyan ate, slept and breathed *Sharpe* for three years, arranging everything, from the supply of props to the control of drivers. As Stepan often remarks, 'Pasha got his grey hairs through *Sharpe*.'

'The Association is a good team,' says Malcolm. 'Stepan will never promise anything unless he knows he can deliver, and in three years, they never let us down once.'

'The locations were magnificent,' remembers Muir. 'We looked at videos of the Sochi area, Western Ukraine, the Carpathian Mountains and locations in the Crimea,' he recalls. 'The great thing about the Crimea is that there are mountains very like the central Guadarrama mountains outside Madrid. And in other parts the land is rocky and barren, just like areas of Spain and Portugal which Sharpe travels through.'

They chose to recce the Crimea, and in particular the area surrounding the famous resort of Yalta.

Production designer Andrew Mollo, whose credits include *The Eagle Has Landed*, *Dr Zhivago*, *Night of the Generals*, *The Spy That Came In From the Cold* and *Pascali's Island* began to assess the logistics of constructing sets there. He travelled to Yalta and Simferopol, which was to be the second production base in the Ukraine, to recce locations at Beketovo, Eskikermen, Opolznevoye, the Baidar Valley, Dimerdji and Livadia.

While he did so, Andrew drew on his extensive historical knowledge to add useful background information. Thus, in amongst his notes on the best place to construct a bridge or build a fort would be a brief aside about the social life of women in 19th century Spain, or some historical detail on the bathroom etiquette of the period. From the outset, nothing ever happened in a *Sharpe* film without at least four historical experts having thought about it first.

The mighty Russian film industry, though in decline, still had much to offer: world-class cinematographers; costumes from classic films such as *Waterloo* and *War And Peace*; a prop-making department capable of running up tents, camp furniture and cannon overnight, and literally battalions of army recruits from the Ukranian armed forces.

In the event, John Mollo found that much of the promised wardrobe stocks proved to be illusory or in such a poor state of repair that they could not be used. And while the construction workers built fast and well, they were hampered by very limited supplies of materials. So much so that Andrew had to supply numerous items from the West, from waterproof paint to brass fittings for furniture.

The stunt men and special effects people – so crucial to high quality action adventure – were particularly impressive. Malcolm and Muir needed stunt men capable of falling from galloping horses, abseiling down a rock face, loading muskets, fighting, falling into water from bridges, being hanged and being dragged behind horses. They auditioned squads of them, finally settling on a team led by Sasha Philatove, Slava Burlachko and Oleg Keratin.

'We'd never seen stunts of such bravery,' remembers Malcolm. 'We'd never seen stunt men fall from such heights, or onto such hard ground.' In the months to come, these guys would be queuing up to throw themselves off the walls of Badajoz and when a British actor was directed to kick them in sensitive parts of their anatomy, they made it a point of honour not to wear boxes.

'The ingenuity of their special effects guys was incredible,' Malcolm adds. 'They handle explosions very well, and what they lack in materials is more than compensated for by their ingenuity and sheer determination to succeed. In fact, they did the job so well we took them to Turkey. We wouldn't be without them.'

But of course nothing's perfect. One of the problems of the Crimea is that there is an almost complete absence of rivers, and consequently almost no bridges. That was a drawback for *Sharpe*, which needs both. Another was that there were very few old buildings in that area, and those there are are usually too close to modern buildings to be usable. The cost of construction, therefore, was going to be considerable.

But overriding all else was the concern about whether the Russian facilities could deliver on time.

'There's a tradition of great cinematography in Russia,' says Malcolm. 'But their films take literally years to make. Under the old regime, what mattered was the quality of the film and the message, and they didn't care much about how long it took to make, or how much it cost.'

'In the UK it's very different. Money is the imperative which rules all film-making in this country. We're used to shooting a film in 30 days, working from 8am to 7pm, six days a week, travelling one or two hours a day. We're forced into it by the economics, particularly

Set construction on 'Sharpe', literally a monumental task: the Torrecastro set built at Dimerdji in the Ukraine in 1992 is still standing

with a production like *Sharpe*, where it's on a knife edge the whole time. In short, if *Sharpe* was to go there, we had to be sure they could operate like that.'

Malcolm and Muir put together a handpicked team of highly experienced people to make the shows. Director Jim Goddard, director of photography, Ivan Strasburg, sound recordist Christian Wangler, first assistant director Marc Jenny and associate producer Neville Thompson were all key appointments. Getting the finances right was equally important, and since these were to be probably the biggest action adventure films ever attempted on British television, in addition to the right team, they needed solid financial guarantees:

'The reason we went to Russia was because we could do it there at the right price,' says Malcolm. 'But we wouldn't have done it without two things: first, a very rigorous completion guarantor to confirm it was viable, and most importantly – the Association. Because it was half owned by Central, it was a big comfort factor: if the Russians failed to deliver, I could say they'd failed me, not vice versa.'

The decision was made to go ahead. Instantly, the great monster that is a film production machine swung into action. Huge amounts of resources were mobilised to build the village of Torrecastro at Dimerdji. A Russian technical crew some 80-strong, with 20 assistants, 67 drivers and several interpreters was taken on. The convoy of 80 vehicles – some of which were there to be cannibalised for spares – was arranged. Three hundred extras from the Ukranian army, and 40 horsemen, were signed up to play the British and French soldiers.

Meanwhile casting went ahead in Britain, and a shortlist was drawn up for the leading role. On it were Rufus Sewell, Clive Owen and Mark McGann. Sean Bean was not available at the time: having recently completed *Patriot Games*, he was by then working on *Lady Chatterly*.

As it turned out, none of them got the part, and in August 1992, it was the slim, dark, finely featured Paul McGann, star of *Withnail And I*, *The Monocled Mutineer* and *Paper Mask*, who boarded the flight to Moscow.

With him were 30 other British, French and Spanish actors, all of them armed with home comforts they'd been told were unavailable in the Ukraine. The list of things to bring issued by production co-ordinator Winnie Wishart was not short: tea, coffee, dried milk, Horlicks, Cup-a-Soup, biscuits, cheese, nuts, dried fruit, chocolate, chewing gum, mineral water, soft drinks, toilet rolls, tissues, aspirin, deodorant, soap (for use and as gifts), toothpaste (and, of course, toothbrush), Dettol, tights (also for use as gifts), batteries, torch, zip-lock plastic bags, first aid kit, Swiss army knife, sewing kit and safety pins, Sellotape and Super Glue, scissors, a flask, cigarettes, videos, small US dollar bills, condoms, tampons, umbrellas, a universal bath plug and a good book. And that's just an excerpt! Having seen that list, no-one was in any doubt that they were off to uncharted territory.

For Malcolm, the biggest anxiety was whether the Russians would all be there on the first day. He knew that just two or three absences would be enough to prevent filming.

To Malcolm's delight, filming began on time, but two days later, one small event changed the course of the series.

Cast and crew were enjoying a well-deserved rest at the beach, and someone suggested a game of football. Among those who got up to play was Paul. A keen footballer and extremely fit, Paul hadn't even made contact with the ball when onlookers were alarmed to see him suddenly gasp with pain and fall to the ground in agony.

He had injured the cruciate ligament in his left knee. With barely 10 minutes of the first film in the can, the leading actor was on crutches.

A doctor was flown out from London, treatment was prescribed, and Paul limped bravely back to work. Schedules were re-arranged to shoot the few scenes he wasn't in, and then again so that he could shoot his least strenuous scenes first. But five weeks later, there were no scenes left in which he didn't have to run, jump or fight, and he was still in pain.

At a tense meeting of cast and crew, Malcolm announced that after discussion with Central, he was halting production and declaring *force majeure* – all contracts terminated due to circumstances beyond his control.

Six years – and two and a half million pounds – after the project had first begun, the majority of the Western cast and crew flew back to London. *Sharpe* had again come to an end. The next few days passed in an agony of uncertainty. It would be four months before Paul could safely work again. Would Central – and more to the point, its insurance company – be prepared to wait?

The insurers were sympathetic. Even before the team had left

Yalta, a series of urgent telephone calls to London had alerted casting director John Hubbard to the problem. Could he find a new lead? John rang Sean Bean, always his first choice for *Sharpe*, and as luck would have it, he was free. Within two days, a contract was signed. Less than eight days after the team had left Yalta, not knowing if they would ever see it again, they were back.

Along with Sean, there were two other new members of the team. The first was director Tom Clegg, veteran of four and a half years of *The Sweeney* as well as episodes of *Between the Lines*, *Boon* and *Minder*, who replaced Jim Goddard.

The second was Assumpta Serna, the Spanish actress, who was replacing Diana Penalvar in the role of the fiery partisan leader, Teresa.

Paul's accident had effects that went far beyond the changes to the cast list. Firstly, it triggered an insurance claim of £2,128,172 – the biggest in British television history – which represented the cost of re-shooting and re-scheduling the films.

Secondly, it meant losing a film. The cruel Russian winter was closing in fast, and if *Rifles* was to be re-shot, one of the other films would have to go. It was *Gold*, the third of the scripts. When that book was finally filmed, in the third year of *Sharpe*, it was with a new script, new characters and a substantially different plot.

If the alternative was losing the production altogether, that seemed a small price to pay. Miraculously, *Sharpe* was back on course.

Tom Clegg directs his leading actor: 'Sean is Sharpe'

Sharpe's Battles

Each 'Sharpe' film takes an army of cast, crew and extras 30 days to shoot. The schedule is tight, and the pace relentless, but the result is big-screen values on the small screen.

CHAPT

3

BATTLES

It is night-time, and very cold. A small group of men wearing the dark green jackets of Riflemen go through a ditch, then scramble up the battered walls of a fortress towards the waiting French. Ahead of them are the guns and bayonets of the enemy; behind them, the guns and bayonets of their comrades. But still they go forward.

The sound of gunfire peppers the air, mingled with the cries of wounded men. The French stab and slash at them, and the Riflemen fight back, every inch of ground paid for in blood and sweat. Everywhere there is smoke and confusion. Explosions, fires, the stink of battle. As men fall, others take their place. And still they go forward.

'It looks great on screen, but on set you can't see more than about two metres ahead of you half the time,' says Lyndon Davies, alias Rifleman Perkins. 'At night, the horses literally come out of the darkness at you. You hear their hooves before you see them, there's mud flying everywhere and you get this surge of adrenaline. You really feel that you're there.'

That the actors themselves feel they're in the thick of battle is

The Dimerdji area in the Crimea doubled for the Guadarrama mountains in Central Spain

a tribute to director Tom Clegg, stunt co-ordinator Dinny Powell, Russian stunt master Sasha Philatove, and special effects supervisor, Goby Evitsky.

The main sword fights are choreographed in meticulous detail. 'Sean's done some excellent fights,' says Dinny. 'He's very fit and he does all his own stunts. You don't have to hold his hand. The Chosen Men are also very good, especially Jason. With Jason, you've got to hold him back. He'd do anything.'

The team plans the position and timing of each explosion, where cavalry and extras will be, and where the riderless horses are supposed to go. Before every take, each actor is shown his particular path through the mêlée, and there is a rehearsal. Says Lyndon, 'You have to know where you're going so that you can both act and watch out for your own safety. But when it comes down to it, the battles are so realistic, you don't have to act. You just run. Sean leads, and we just follow.'

Jason Salkey (right) and a Russian stuntman, showing that acting is very much a contact sport

Wellington and Nairn survey the bloody aftermath of the Siege of Badajoz. The assault took 14 freezing nights to film

As in all his films, in 'Sharpe' Sean insists on doing all his own stunts. 'I enjoy doing it, it's part of the job. And it always looks better'

ACCIDENTS

ven the most static television programme can go wrong, but in high-action shows like *Sharpe*, the potential for accidents – and therefore the concern for safety – is correspondingly greater.

Ironically, the most serious accidents have happened off-camera. In one case a French actor came close to losing his eye when someone turned round and cut him with a bayonet in a rehearsal. On another occasion, a chef slipped and fell down some steps at the Rossiya Hotel,

fracturing his skull.

Sean, obviously in the front line a lot of the time, has had many a cut and burn. His closest shave was in *Sharpe's Regiment* when he was crouching in a ditch as a horse thundered overhead. Suddenly, the edge of the ditch gave way, and one of the horse's rear legs threw up a clod of earth which hit him on the head. Although he wrenched his shoulder badly, it was a lucky escape: another inch, and he would have been crushed.

TOM CLEGG — DIRECTOR

The dynamo that drives each day's shoot is director Tom Clegg. Working on the principle that if he sits down, everyone sits down, he simply doesn't. The result is a set that's fast and efficient.

'*Sharpe* is hugely ambitious for its time,' says Tom. 'After *The Jewel In The Crown* and *Brideshead Revisited*, the prevailing view within the industry was that never again would we be able to attempt drama on this scale. *Sharpe* has proved that we can.'

Tom is delighted to have proved the sceptics wrong.

Having directed 14 episodes of *The Sweeney*, two of *Between The Lines*, and various episodes of *Boon, Bergerac, Minder, Van De Valk, The Professionals* and *Return Of The Saint*, he knows a thing or two about action-adventure.

'Action isn't just about fights,' says Tom. 'Action is what moves the story on dramatically. Hemingway once said "Do not confuse movement with action", which is another way of saying that just because people are rushing around doesn't make it action. A good argument between Sharpe and Hakeswill can have as much action as the Chosen Men running across a battlefield.'

Tom admits that *Sharpe* is very male-orientated. 'It has to be. The essence of these films is war, and war was about men. But that doesn't mean they don't appeal to women.'

Part of what appeals to women is Sharpe's relationship with Harper: 'It allows Sharpe to escape the confines of the major plot, to make that move back to being one of the men, to be vulnerable,' he explains. 'Also, it allows us to bring humour in, and show the loyalty between men, and the value of a huge friendship.'

Sharpe's Regiment, says Tom, is especially interesting. 'For the first time we're able to bring Sharpe back to England where he was born, taking him through a huge range of locations and dramatic roles. This has given Sean the opportunity for a far greater range of emotion, from showing Sharpe's discomfort in the presence of aristocracy to his feelings about going back to the slums where he grew up.' *Sharpe's Justice*, also set in England, further explores his feelings about civilian life.

Tom is clearly a man who enjoys his work: 'Where else would I get the chance to play with all these toys? The guns, the horses, the fights...I love doing *Sharpe*. I've been offered other projects, and having done four years of *Sharpe*, I did wonder whether it was time to take a breather. But I love doing them. I wouldn't want anybody else to do them.'

S T U N T S

ith 30 years experience of co-ordinating stunts, Dinny Powell says he's rarely come across such co-operative actors as those on *Sharpe*.

'Sean and Alice (Krige) fell off a horse once. They were both on the one horse, crossing a stream, and it was very cold. The water was bitterly cold too, and of course, they fell off. They got up and played the whole scene again, Alice with hardly anything on, and both of them blue with cold.'

Dinny is careful not to let the horses get hurt. 'These days there are a lot of things you can't do. For instance, you're not allowed to trip a horse up to make it fall: you can only have horses that fall on command.' In *Sharpe*, very few horses actually fall: mostly they're travelling and it's the stunt rider that comes off. 'And that's just as it should be,' says Dinny. 'Nobody – human or horse – should get hurt for a bit of celluloid.'

But of course stunt men are paid for doing exactly that, and the 11-strong Russian team positively relish it. These men run, jump, fall from horses, dive off walls, and go through fire

Russian stuntmen in 'Sharpe's Enemy': 'The kind of blokes who think that if they haven't been hurt, they haven't been to work'

A Turkish stunt horse gallops past an explosion in 'Sharpe's Mission' - but it's the stuntman who takes the fall

Dinny Powell demonstrates a smash on stuntman Kirill Chevkine

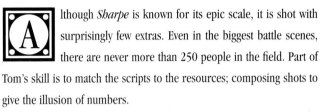

to make the battles look realistic.

'They're very fit and strong, and they have a lot of nerve,' says Dinny. 'They ride well and they don't complain. You have to take care of them, because if they get hurt, they won't let you know.'

The sheer toughness of the Russian stuntmen is breathtaking. Says Lyndon: 'You'd bash them over the head with a rifle and they'd tell you to hit them harder. They're the kind of blokes who think that if they haven't been hurt, they haven't been to work.'

Although *Sharpe* is known for its epic scale, it is shot with surprisingly few extras. Even in the biggest battle scenes, there are never more than 250 people in the field. Part of Tom's skill is to match the scripts to the resources; composing shots to give the illusion of numbers.

In the Ukraine, the extras consisted of 225 army conscripts, trained and organised by Richard Moore, the show's military adviser. His detailed knowledge of the period, skill at making and fixing weapons, and ability to turn a mass of undisciplined army cadets – not to mention actors – into battle-hardened soldiers, is unsurpassed. The Chosen Men first met Richard in London in the summer of 1992. 'At first he seemed a bit weird,' remembers Lyndon. 'He arrived at the rehearsal room in full Rifleman's uniform, which he'd worn all the way there on the train from Sheffield.' After briefing the actors on conditions in Wellington's army and how best to make their portrayals convincing, Richard asked if anyone was going back on the underground, 'Suddenly,' says Lyndon, 'everyone wanted to take the bus.'

After a few days of intensive training at a firing range in West

Sean and fellow actors learnt to handle guns authentically from Richard Moore, historical advisor for all 14 'Sharpe' films to date

Russian stuntmen give their all again - this time as French cavalry doomed to defeat at Sharpe's hands

Sean is skilled in several kinds of swordplay: here he duels with Francois Guetary in 'Sharpe's Enemy'

London, Richard had taught the Chosen Men not only how to load, fire and carry arms, but also how the army was organised, how the Rifles operated and what it was like to be a soldier. He then went to the Crimea to teach the Ukrainian extras the same things. The entry in his diary documenting his first impression of the Ukrainian recruits – and what he takes to be their first impression of him – speaks volumes:

'From beneath an oversized furry Russian chapska, a pair of tiny red-rimmed eyes peeped out, pensive and scared. Who was this lunatic in the unrecognisable green uniform and shiny top boots, smoking a cigar with his mittened hands clenched behind his back, looking like a cross between Stalin and Napoleon?'

They soon found out. And despite their initial reluctance to be in the film, they were won over by the promise of decent treatment – in normal service they get little to eat, are paid less and are perpetually cold – and plenty of western cigarettes. They were repaid by Richard's constant support and encouragement – albeit sometimes hidden under the bark of orders – and his endless attempts to get them decent food and cigarettes.

Richard, who learnt enough Russian to drill them in their own language, describes the training process as one of de-brainwashing.

'I began by talking to them, and giving them cigarettes, and I treated them like an army. When they were in period dress, they were my responsibility, and because they had so little in life, I kept them in it as much as possible.'

At times, life in Wellington's army must have seemed little better than life in their own army. While some soldiers worked as extras, others were hired to build roads to get the unit vehicles to the less accessible locations; some also repaired the huge sets when they were damaged by gale-force winds.

Filming the Siege of Badajoz in *Sharpe's Company* was the hardest time of all. 'The weather was appalling,' says Richard. 'Fourteen nights of heavy frost and sleet, and an average temperature of minus 2. The lads were blue with cold, some were injured, and some were cracking up at the emotional intensity of it.' Richard is full of admiration for the men who have fought for *Sharpe*, and particularly those who stormed the breach at Badajoz.

ARMOURERS

e had less respect for the Russian armourers. 'When we arrived, they didn't know anything about muzzle loaders or even what a flintlock is,' he remembers. 'Their swords were rusty, muskets bunged up with old cloth, and the Russian gunpowder was weak.' To his horror, he once discovered one of them sticking his finger down the barrel of a loaded pistol.

British armourers William J. Whitlam and Tom Moriarty have a far more professional approach. A tall, gangly fellow whose job is to handle, fire and guard the weapons, like Richard, Will's solemn face is often to be found glaring at the camera from beneath the shako of a rifleman.

Filming *Sharpe's Regiment* in England was very different from the Ukrainian experience. This time the South Essex were re-enactors recruited from the ranks of the Napoleonic Association. Their devotion to accuracy and their superb drill and stamina adds much to the realism of these scenes.

Richard printed recruiting posters calling them to arms: 'Arouse Britons for the Honour and Glory of Olde England!,' they read. 'Chastise the Perfidious French! Never want for

RICHARD MOORE — MILITARY ADVISOR

Richard Rutherford Moore spent his childhood with his nose pressed up against the glass cabinets of displays in military museums. At 15, he applied to join the Duke of Wellington's Regiment, the 33rd Foot – coincidentally Sharpe's first regiment – but was told to come back on his 16th birthday. By that time, however, he'd been in a motorcycle accident and was deemed unfit.

Although he's not a fighting soldier, soldiering is still his life's work. A long-standing member of the Napoleonic Association, whose members re-enact battles of the period, Richard describes himself as 'an experienced muzzle-loading rifle and pistol shooter, who writes prodigiously, and lives in the eighteenth century.'

Richard believes that hands-on experience is the only way to really understand weapons, and he's been known to fire muskets in lectures, setting off smoke alarms and calling the fire brigade. But he is unrepentant.

'Words alone can't tell you what it was like.'

He brings the same fidelity to his work on *Sharpe*. Not only did he recruit the re-enactors, but he ate, marched and fought with them

Military and historical advisor, Richard Moore

too. 'I'd never ask them to do anything I wouldn't do myself,' says Richard simply. Thus on the English shoot, while softer souls were tucked up warmly in their hotel beds, Richard and the re-enactors were sleeping in tents on the locations.

In the Ukraine, keen to extend his knowledge of contemporary military matters, Richard spent an illicit night in Simferopol Barracks when the extras went back after work. Smuggled past the guards by his new-found friends, he explored the huge, cold barracks with awe. The soldiers sleep 32 to a room, many of whose windows were broken, and whose doors had long ago been burned for firewood. There was hot water only twice a week, and never enough food. It was a salutary experience.

Small wonder, then, that the soldiers would take every opportunity to get extra food. Richard recalls shooting the scene in which Sharpe tries to enforce Wellington's order that all food and drink must be paid for. Ironically, he says, at that very moment the soldiers of the South Essex were in some nearby orchards – stealing peaches.

Even stuntmen have their limits: dummy heads stand in for dead deserters in 'Sharpe's Enemy'

Courage in this Noble Regiment of BRITISH VOLUNTEERS!'

They had another reason for enlisting, he says: 'All are *Sharpe* devotees who answered the call to give something in return for the enjoyment they've had from the films.'

In Turkey, however, the South Essex was largely comprised of ordinary civilians recruited by means of small ads in the papers, a TV appearance and several illegally fly-posted recruitment posters. After a training day thwarted by lateness, lists and no lunch, the initial 400 were soon whittled down to a more manageable 200. Since neither bullets nor muskets had arrived, they had to be taught to drill using pinecones and camel prods.

'The Turkish boys have stamina and haven't been through the dehumanising process the Ukrainian soldiers had,' says Richard. 'They are quick to react and ask questions – so many, in fact, that along with the drill commands, I rapidly learnt the Turkish for "Shut up!".'

Although Richard is a stickler for historical accuracy, the producers have allowed a degree of dramatic licence to suit the medium. Thus, although the real Duke of Wellington was known to insist on high standards of uniform and discipline among his officers, the team made Sharpe a rebel and a street fighter. Tom explains:

'What's essential is a strong leading character people can identify with,' he says. 'This is a historical piece and it has to be historically accurate, but the visual image is also important. We didn't want Sean to be bogged down with irrelevant historical accuracies which would get in the way of his characterisation.'

'We are conscious whenever we are breaking the rules. There were letters flying around from military purists saying Sharpe must wear his shako, shave, button his jacket before he goes in front of an officer, and so on. But by and large I ignored them.'

Battles are an inevitable part of the action in *Sharpe*, and because the films go out before the 9 o'clock watershed, great care is taken to see that the depiction of violence remains within the limits laid down by the regulators.

The rules say that you can't show any act deemed to be replicable on British streets. Of course the definitions are vague. Orthodox martial violence with swords, muskets and pistols seems to be acceptable: but strangling, knifings and hangings aren't. Tom admits to a certain frustration with this.

'If the show was going out between 9 and 11pm we would have a truer representation of what war was like at that time. But there's no point in wasting time doing things which are

THE PENINSULAR WAR

The Peninsular War was Britain's principal land action during the Napoleonic War and was fought for control of Spain and Portugal after the Spanish rebelled against the rule of Joseph Bonaparte, Napoleon's brother. (The titles of key *Sharpe* films are given in brackets indicating the historical point at which they are set: these sometimes differ from the corresponding novels.)

- **VIMEIRO** – 17 August 1808: Wellesley beat off a French attack but orders from a superior officer forbade him to press his advantage and take Lisbon.

- **CORUÑA** – 16-18 January, 1809: Following a gruelling march in the depths of winter, pursued by Napoleon, Sir John Moore and 29,000 men boarded ships home. Although his infantry defeated the pursuing Marshal Soult, Moore himself was mortally wounded. (*Sharpe's Rifles*)

- **TALAVERA** – 27-28 July 1809: A French attack on Sir Arthur Wellesley's troops was repelled. (*Sharpe's Eagle*). See map on page 142.

- **BUSACO** – 17 September 1810: Anglo-Portuguese forces give the French a bloody nose before retiring into the secret Lines of Torres Vedras.

- **FUENTES D'ONORO** – 3-5 May 1811: 37,000 British and Portuguese troops narrowly escaped defeat at the hands of 48,000 French.

- **ALBUERA** – 16 May 1811: The French retained Badajoz, then under siege by Sir William Beresford, but at huge cost. (The novel *Sharpe's Battle* is set in this period, the film is set some two years later.)

- **THE SIEGES OF CIUDAD RODRIGO AND BADAJOZ** – January–April 1812: Wellington overcame both fortresses. (*Sharpe's Company*). See map on page 143.

- **SALAMANCA** – 22 July 1812: British and Portuguese soldiers under Wellington conquered a force under Marshal Marmount, opening the way to Madrid. (*Sharpe's Enemy*)

- **VITORIA** – 21 June 1813: The British exacted a decisive victory over the French. (The films *Sharpe's Honour*, *Gold* and *Sword* were set during this period, although the book of *Gold* was set during Torres Vedras (1810-11) and *Sword* at Salamanca.)

- **NIVELLES** – 1813: Wellington crossed the River Nives and forced the French to evacuate their base at Bayonne.

- **BATTLES OF THE PYRENEES** – September-November 1813: Wellington swept into France. (*Sharpe's Regiment*, *Mission* and *Siege*)

- **ORTHEZ** – February 1814: The French were forced to retreat. Wellington suffered his only wound of the war.

- **TOULOUSE** – April 1814: Wellington crossed the River Garonne, took the Calvinet Ridge and was about to lay siege to the highly fortified military base at Toulouse when news of Napoleon's abdication arrived. (*Sharpe's Revenge*)

- **WATERLOO** – 18 June 1815: Napoleon and Wellington met in battle. Napoleon was defeated. (*Sharpe's Waterloo*). See map on page 126.

Producer Malcolm Craddock (left of camera), director of photography Ivan Strasburg (behind camera) and director Tom Clegg (behind Ivan)

going to be censored afterwards.'

The creative considerations involved in making *Sharpe* were one thing: the practicalities were something else again. *Sharpe* was conceived during the last days of communism in the former USSR, and the chaos that ensued inevitably affected the ability of the East West Creative Association to service the production.

As the Association's Igor Nossov sagely observes, the old system had its disadvantages, but at least you knew where you were:

'In those days, if your film ran into problems, you could appeal to the leaders for help, and they would throw in all the resources. But times have changed. And for film-makers, they've changed for the worse.'

Igor's role is to maintain high level contacts throughout the army, the government and even the Mafia to keep their production on the rails. He jokes that he sometimes had to reverse perestroika to get *Sharpe* made:

'In the first year we made *Sharpe*, there were no Ukrainian customs, so we could bring in whatever supplies we needed from anywhere in the USSR. Later, customs got more difficult, so we had to find supplies within the Ukraine. This is when we had to get in touch with the Mafia because everything which is in short supply is always under the control of the Mafia.'

Petrol was also hard to find. As the Crimea struggled for independence from the Ukraine, Russia exerted leverage by starving the Ukraine of oil. The resulting fuel shortage required the Association to import petrol from Russia – with associated pay-offs to interested parties.

Like a good Russian, Igor does his networking in the sauna.

'It's good to talk to the bigshots when they are naked,' he laughs. 'That's when the barriers come down.'

Sauna diplomacy was required with a general of the Ukrainian army during the second year's filming.

'The general showed me a piece of paper which he said could seriously affect relations with *Sharpe*. I asked him "What is this paper?" He said, "It's a report from one of my intelligence officers about how the British are buying items of military uniform from the army. A copy has been sent to Kiev, and Kiev has recommended that the soldiers are removed." I knew this was very serious: if the soldiers were withdrawn, the production would collapse. So I asked the general what he was going to do with the paper. "It's very simple," says the general. "That intelligence officer is a colonel. But he's always making trouble, so now he will become a captain again. We'll say the soldiers gave the items to the British as presents, and we'll put this paper in the fire." And he did so.'

Igor's contacts came in handy many times, but never more so than in October 1993. It was during the putsch and the Ukrainian minister of defence ordered all soldiers to return to barracks and be ready for action.

'This was a disaster. *Sharpe* was filming a huge battle scene in the Baidar Valley, and winter was approaching. They couldn't have stopped.'

So Igor took a plane to Kiev and managed to get a meeting with the head of the General Staff.

'I told him that if we take the army away from the locations, the British journalists will write in their papers that the Ukraine is preparing for a military conflict. That will be very bad for us, just for the sake of getting 200 soldiers to barracks. He picked up the phone and cancelled the orders.'

Natural disasters might also have jeopardised production. In November the previous year, a fluke hurricane had swept across the Crimea without warning and destroyed older houses in Yalta, felled many trees, and carried several ships out to sea.

In Dimerdji, half way up the mountains, the set was in some disarray, and under four inches of snow – something of a handicap

Ukrainian recruits served as extras, security guards and road builders during the first three years of 'Sharpe'

given that the action then being shot was supposed to take place in high summer in Spain!

Once again, the Association fell back on the army. While some soldiers began repairs, others set up a team to clear the snow and ice from the set using a traditional Russian method of fighting the snow: salt. They bought up the salt supplies from all the restaurants in Yalta, and every day for a week, the team went to the set two hours early and cleared it of snow. And to melt any recalcitrant bits of ice, they used the more modern technology of flame throwers.

The army also fulfiled other roles. On location, the electrical demands of the production were met by huge army generators whose powerful engines and enormous wheels meant they could reach the most awkward of locations. They also have surprisingly quiet motors, which is a boon to film-makers. Army personnel-carriers ferried cast and crew to inaccessible locations, and if a vehicle had mechanical difficulties, the drivers would spend hours extracting the offending engine from the vehicle, stripping it down and fixing it.

At night the empty sets were watched over by army extras who slept in tents nearby. Stepan and Igor arranged for petrol to be brought in by tanker from Finland and Germany, and protected it with an armed guard provided by the soldiers.

On location in the Ukraine with 'Sharpe': grip Philip Jones moves the camera

SET CONSTRUCTION

everal large sets designed by Andrew Mollo, the production designer, were constructed for *Sharpe*, and it is a testimony to the craftsmanship of the Russian workers that some of them still stand to this day.

'*Sharpe* is a marvellous opportunity for a designer because you get the opportunity to build really big sets,' says Andrew. 'Most design work for television these days is domestic sets, prison interiors and the odd hospital. But with *Sharpe*, each script required a village or fort or a huge bridge.'

Not only that, but no-one had done it there before. 'Making *Sharpe* in the Ukraine made us feel like pioneers,' he says. 'And it's quite ironic that in 1965, I recreated Russia in Spain for *Dr Zhivago*, and nearly 30 years later, there I was in the Ukraine, recreating Spain.'

'The big build in the first year was Torrecastro town. That was difficult because we had to learn the system from scratch. We didn't know what materials were available, or how long things took to do. And of course the soviet system is quite complex and bureaucratic, and it was difficult to work out how to get things done or how to change them once they were done.'

That first year saw a short trip to Portugal at the end of the shoot where Lisbon-based producers Patricia Vieira and Jose Correia located the interiors that had been unavailable in the Ukraine. The grand Louis XIV rooms of the Post Master General's office at Loures, near Lisbon, doubled for the officers' mess and Wellington's HQ, and the farmhouse scenes in which Sharpe and Teresa first meet were filmed nearby. The same team co-ordinated a short shoot for *Sharpe* two years later.

1993 was the year of the really big builds – Badajoz and the monastery. 'We knew the ropes by then, but there was a lot more to do,' says Andrew. And though the crew got better, economic conditions in the Ukraine were getting worse.

Badajoz was particularly complex. It involved building a wall 11 metres high and 50 metres long, capable of bearing the weight of dozens of extras. A scale model of the siege works was also built: this was the size of a small room.

Construction was comparatively light in the third year, and the French Fort largely involved alterations to existing sets. In the fourth year of filming, however, it was back to work with a vengeance. This was the biggest build of all – only this time, it was in Turkey.

Wardrobe on this production was a huge job, and Andrew's brother John had his work cut out designing the costumes and deciding which should be hired, which made – and where. The principals' costumes, along with the uniforms of the British soldiers, were made by the

Full-size sets of the walls of Badajoz - seen here through wicker 'gabbions' - were also used with scale models of the town

renowned theatrical costume supplier, Angels. The French uniforms were either hired from, or made at, various Russian film studios, particularly Mosfilm in Moscow, under the veteran Russian wardrobe mistress, Helen Khramova.

One memo from Helen gives a glimpse of the huge scale of the operation: 110 French infantry tunics, 100 rough grey trousers, 100 rough white trousers, 100 shirts, 121 shakos... the list is endless.

In a country already too poor to feed its own people, and now wracked by social and political unrest, the task of supplying the needs of a huge Western cast and crew was a mammoth one. It was a task that fell to the East-West Creative Association, led by Stepan Pojenian, and on a day-to-day basis to Pavel Douvidson. Finding locations, building the sets, making props and costumes, arranging accommodation, hiring transport, finding equipment, extras, horses and explosives – and the technicians to use them – liaising with studios, and organising food and water were Pavel's responsibilities.

Inevitably, on such a huge undertaking, there were misunderstandings. Generally these arose because of the very different film-making cultures of the two countries. And although the Association did a magnificent job under trying circumstances, it could not change the habits of a lifetime overnight.

Despite inevitable setbacks, production still cracks on at a fearsome rate. Each two-hour *Sharpe* film is shot in 30 days, which necessitates – according to director of photography Chris O'Dell – around 30 set-ups a day. Considering the amount of action shots, and the small number of interiors in most *Sharpe* films, this is a relentless pace. It's especially pressured for members of the Russian crew who traditionally produce films more slowly.

In Russia, people are used to taking a year to make a film. Each year, the *Sharpe* team arrived in the Ukraine determined to make three in 17 weeks. In Russia, one defends oneself from blame by refusing to take responsibility for making decisions. In the West, film-making depends on well-defined areas of responsibility and clear lines of communication.

Julian Fellowes as Maj. Dunnett in 'Rifles' (above); he also plays Prinny in 'Regiment' (see p 102)

Mixing the two cultures is not straightforward, as second assistant director Sam Craddock explains: 'In Britain, we estimate that filming costs about £60,000 a day, so every minute you go over schedule costs a lot of money. In Russia, money – and therefore time – has never been the problem. In Britain, when you ask how long it will take to get something ready, you'd get a precise estimate. In Russia, they'd invariably say, "As long as it takes".'

A typical day for Sam entailed getting up at 4am, getting on set at 6am, working all day, and going back to the hotel at 8pm to write reports and distribute the call sheet. After supper, he'd go to bed, getting up at 2 am to change the batteries on the walkie talkies, and getting up again at 4 am. As production co-ordinator Tatyana Shakhgeldyan explains, the Russian crew found it very strange to see the British 'work their buttocks off' as a matter of course.

'We do it when there's an emergency,' she says frankly. 'But these people were doing it 14 hours a day, six days a week.'

Because of the shortages of materials in Russia, advance warning is required to obtain almost anything.

'Russians don't understand our habit of making up our minds at the last moment,' adds Andrew. 'If you want 50 horses, you have to specify 50 horses about 12 weeks in advance. And if you then only want 40 horses, it'll be as much bother as if you'd suddenly asked for 60.'

Equally ingrained is the Russian tendency to ignore an impending problem in the hope that it would go away.

'If the 50 horses are late, the Russian crew won't tell you until the last moment, hoping that the problem will resolve itself in the interim,' says Andrew. 'You have to check up all the time.'

Such communications problems were anathema to a French first assistant director such as Marc Jenny. A talented organiser, and the person who bore the responsibility of scheduling production, Marc depended on swift communication of problems to run the shoot, and when he didn't get it, the guilty party would be treated to a glimpse of his fiery Gallic temper.

The carefully-constructed illusion that there are vast numbers of soldiers is part of what gives the 'Sharpe' films their epic feel . . .

... *Yet even in 'Sharpe's' biggest battle scenes, there are never more than 250 extras in the field*

A Ukrainian extra takes time off from his role as a French infantryman. The previous day he had been a British redcoat

The Russians could be equally volatile, and the drivers were a law unto themselves. In Russia, anyone who has a vehicle has power, and with up to 80 vehicles in use by the production, and fuel in very short supply, it was vital to keep the drivers happy.

Organising interpreters was 'a bit like running a dating agency,' says the Association's Caroline McManus. 'You need to choose people who have the appropriate experience for each department. It's very easy for highly qualified people to feel that they're being bossed around by a mere interpreter.'

It was particularly difficult for women. Says Malcolm, 'The female interpreters didn't have authority with the drivers. We had to make clear to the drivers that the interpreters spoke with my authority, so to ignore them was to ignore me.'

Being ignored isn't an option for sound recordist Christian Wangler: without silence, he can't do his job, but because Russian film makers don't record sound direct but dub it on later, a Russian set is never quiet. One of the many tasks of the first assistant director is to get the set quiet for a take, but Christian's always ready to help out: 'I put six rocks on the sound table,' he says with a wicked grin. 'So far, I've never had to throw one.'

Despite these difficulties, Christian is renowned for getting high quality dialogue, and throughout his four years on the show, he has very rarely had to resort to re-recording dialogue. Christian attributes his skill in this regard to his training in documentaries where very often you get it right first time, or you don't get it at all.

Good quality dialogue helps give the films their cinematic feel. In the dub, as many as 100 separate sound tracks are used to achieve the rich audio quality, and this – together with the fact that it is shot 'wide-screen' on Super-16 – is part of what makes *Sharpe* feel filmic rather than simply televisual.

But while some people struggled endlessly with the unfamiliar, certain others seemed to be able to bridge the two cultures spontaneously. Even without fluent Russian, associate producer Neville Thompson was immensely popular with the Russian production office. 'His tact, patience and wisdom made the production not only possible, but fun,' says Tatyana. Andrew Mollo was another person whose genial good humour and endless patience led the Russians to regard him as one of their own.

Malcolm is keenly aware that the Russians have many good qualities. 'Lots of our Russian friends are very well educated, and have read far more Shakespeare and Dickens than I have,' he says. 'They have very strong family values, and although with the new middle class, material things are becoming more important, they still maintain these values which we have really lost.'

'And they really came into their own when we ran into problems. When sets blew down, they re-built them without a murmur, and if a vehicle broke down, they wouldn't think twice about stripping down the engine to get it moving again. When we re-cast *Sharpe* and had to re-build the bridge in *Eagle* so that we could blow it up again, they just did it. To us it was devastating, but to them, it was all in a day's work.'

Andrew Mollo: production designer and honorary Russian, his credits include 'Dr Zhivago' and 'The Eagle Has Landed'

Rain gives make-up artist Jacquetta Levon (left) and hairdresser Sano de Perpessac (right) a chance to check their handiwork

LIVING CONDITIONS

For Westerners, living conditions in the Ukraine were very tough. Simferopol – quickly dubbed 'Simplyawful' – was particularly hard. The days were long, food was short, and at times during the third year, water was desperately scarce. Temperatures ranged from 35 degrees in summer to minus 18 in winter, and accomodation was hardly palatial. In the first year, cast and crew were plagued by a virulent stomach parasite, and in the third, a cholera epidemic in nearby towns caused much anxiety. Telephone contact with home was sporadic and entertainment non-existent.

The resort town of Yalta, where cast and crew were quartered in a KGB sanatorium, was a good deal better. Even so, as economic conditions worsened, it was difficult for a Western cast and crew to feel comfortable, safe and at ease. Despite the problems, the atmosphere was generally cheerful. Everyone was friendly and always keen to see new faces – especially when the new arrival brought video tapes of recent football matches, or was willing to enter into endless tournaments of Risk or chess. And when no other entertainment was

available, people invented their own.

Michael Mears – aka Rifleman Cooper – recalls whiling away a boring afternoon in the rest tent with Sean, Daragh and the Chosen Men by inventing an elaborate version of hoopla. The game involved throwing coathangers onto a clothes rail, and each successive strike provoked roars of approval from the contestants – and a terse message from the set requesting them to keep the noise down. Daragh ran a book, setting himself up as 'William O'Hill, offices throughout the Crimea', and as the afternoon wore on, the Chosen Men lost their shirts – or at least, their *per diems* – on the outcome. Finally, someone issued the ultimate challenge: could Jason Salkey – freestyle Frisbee champion of the universe – hit the rail blindfold? He could, and the cheer which greeted his success earnt the players another stinging rebuke from the first assistant.

Russians are used to being adaptable, but even they concede that the third series of *Sharpe* was carried out under conditions of extraordinary privation. The problems were threefold: water, cholera and Mafia. Although few members of the British team had any dealings with them, the

The Throne Room in 'Sharpe's Regiment': to hire a pile on the scale required for Sharpe costs around £2,500 a day

Mafia – noticable by their large cars and overdressed women – weren't shy.

'The Mafia had really muscled in between the second and third series,' says Chris Burt, who produced the show in its third year. 'In Simferopol, I had to ask the cafes in the hotel to shut down the music several times a night. The reactions varied from total disinterest to having a pistol pointed at my stomach by a drunken Russian.' Whether the people concerned were bona fide Mafia or not is debatable. But whoever they were, they were young, drunk and entirely unpredictable.

Although cholera never reached the set, it came too close for comfort. There were cases in Simferopol after the cast and crew left. But the main problem that year was water. When production began in August 1994, the Ukraine was in the throws of its worst drought for 20 years. All over the Crimea water was either rationed or not available, and queues of locals with empty buckets were common. As Chris notes, 'There were water-bowzers at street level, and cast and crew had to take buckets up to their

rooms to wash with. We were getting drinking water from East Germany, Poland and Greece through various dollar shops, but in Yalta we were down to our last 20 bottles.'

However, following high level meetings with the Crimean authorities, the Association was given permission to draw water from Simferopol's main supply, especially to supply the production in Yalta. As a result, they managed to keep the supply going in the sanatorium for all but one day.

For the core cast, trips home were impossible: even if the schedule hadn't been so packed, it was 22 hours by train to Moscow, and internal flights were frequently cancelled if there was no fuel. Daragh confesses that the old hands such as he and the Chosen Men – who were there for 17 or 18 weeks at a stretch – would smile at the actors who flew in for a couple of weeks and then went home again. 'For them it was an adventure,' he says. 'For us, it was hard work.' By December 1994, some members of the cast were not unhappy to be leaving Yalta for the last time.

Simmerson hides his second battalion. These he found on a small privately owned island in the salt marshes near where Arthur Ransome set his book *Swallows and Amazons*. Horsey Island is ideal for period drama: it has no modern buildings, and no tell-tale electricity pylons and can only be reached by boat or causeway. However, only one of the three films could be shot in England: the others required locations that could pass for Spain and France. But if not in the Ukraine, then where?

The answer was Turkey. The areas around Antalya and Selifke, two towns on the Silk Road, doubled very well for Spain, and the numerous *karavansarai* – stopping places for the caravans – were also used. Malcolm and Muir found a suitable production manager – Ali Akdeniz – who set up the Turkish end of the shoot, and it was close enough to the Crimea for costumes and crew to be shipped over from Yalta without difficulty.

The old town in Antlaya and a nearby nature reserve doubled for areas on the Franco-Spanish border in *Sharpe's Mission*, and after much searching, an ancient ruined castle was found in at Limankalesi near Silifke which fulfilled the requirements for the fort in *Sharpe's Siege*.

But as Andrew explains, it had one drawback: 'The problem was, the gateway had collapsed and there was no way to get inside it.'

The solution was to design walls which could be added onto the castle, and a gateway which led into a courtyard where all the action takes place. By restoring parts of the original battlements, recreating the original gun-ports, strengthening upper floors, and matching existing stonework, Andrew felt he could make it work.

Designing it was one thing, getting it built was quite another.

'We tried to find a Turkish company with set-building experience, but there are none,' says Andrew. 'So I brought over from Yalta one of the construction teams which had built four large sets for the previous three series of *Sharpe*. All their sets had survived three Russian winters, which shows how well-built they are.'

This crew worked for several weeks on the castle set in Selifke, and the site became something of a local tourist attraction for groups of Turkish and German tourists who came to watch the semi-naked Ukrainians clambering all over the set without the help of ladders.

Now that the TV films have come to a natural end, many people are asking whether Sharpe will return to the screen.

'We hope to make a film called *Sharpe's Tiger* for the cinema,' says Muir. 'It's set in India, and takes place before Sharpe goes to the Peninsula. In it, Sharpe does battle with the Sultan Tippoo, and has his first encounter with his enemy, Sgt. Obadiah Hakeswill, and an officer named Lt. William Lawford, who later becomes his lifelong friend.'

Sharpe, it is hoped, will march again.

After the privations of the Ukraine, it was luxury indeed in 1995 to shoot a *Sharpe* film in Britain where most members of cast and crew could stay at home or in decent hotels, be visited by their families, and enjoy normal life. But in logistical terms, shooting in England was no less complex than the Russian shoots.

'The fourth year of *Sharpe* is the most ambitious we've ever undertaken,' says Malcolm. 'Both England and Turkey are totally new countries to us. It took a lot of courage to convince Carlton that we could do *Regiment*. When you look at the logistics of doing one film in England, it's not easy. It's much easier to do three in Turkey, and have one base.'

It is the job of location manager Dennis Firminger to find and gain access to the various settings required in Britain. But stately homes aren't cheap, and to hire a pile on the scale required for *Sharpe* costs around £2,500 a day and involves detailed negotiation as to what can be added, moved or changed to get the right effect. Dennis also had to find marshland to represent the saltwater marshes where Sir Henry

Sharpe's Campaigns

Synopses of all 14 films detail Sharpe's adventures from the day he saved the life of Sir Arthur Wellesley, to his first - and last - sighting of Napoleon at the Battle of Waterloo.

CHAPTER

4

Sharpe's Rifles

PORTUGAL 1809.

NAPOLEON BONAPARTE IS MASTER OF EUROPE.

HIS BROTHER JOSEPH SITS ON THE THRONE OF SPAIN. SIR ARTHUR

WELLESLEY, SOON TO BE LORD WELLINGTON, THE NEW BRITISH

COMMANDER, HAS TAKEN THE CITY OF OPORTO FROM THE FRENCH.

NOW HE RESTS HIS FORCES BEFORE MAKING AN ADVANCE

INTO SPAIN.

 hile out riding near the British camp, Lord Wellesley is set upon by three French cavalrymen. Seeing the attack, Sgt. Richard Sharpe of the second battalion, 95th Rifles, quickly grabs his rifle, and risks his own life to save that of his commander: he shoots one of the assailants, unhorses another and - though wounded - fells the third.

Wellesley rewards Sharpe with a field commission, making him a lieutenant and placing him under the command of his wily Irish spymaster, Major Hogan.

His first mission is to go 100 miles behind enemy lines to locate a missing agent, James Rothschild, last seen at Casa Antiga, who has a bankdraft for badly needed funds. Sharpe is sent to join the search party led by Major Dunnett, and given command of the Rifles, the finest marksmen in the army.

The initial encounter is not promising. Instead of disciplined soldiers, Sharpe finds a gang of louts sleeping off the excesses of the previous night. But there is steel beneath: when Sharpe kicks them awake, Patrick Harper, a huge bear of an Irishman, grabs him by the throat and the others aim their rifles at him.

Like Harper, Sharpe is a street-fighter, and the two men are still at it when Perkins, Dunnett's drummer boy, comes in search of Lt. Sharpe. Realising his opponent is an officer, Harper straightens up, but not before Dunnett and Murray make clear their disapproval of a lieutenant brawling with one of his men. But what else can one expect of a man raised from the ranks?

Harper and his comrades - Cooper, Hagman, Harris and Tongue - share their misgivings. To them, 'proper' officers are born not made. Officers join the army by choice, rather than because they are too poor to do anything else. Harper bides his time until he can get rid of Sharpe.

Before he can do so, the search party is attacked by Colonel de L'Eclin. Though many - including Dunnett himself - are killed, Sharpe manages to keep the Rifles alive, and rescues young Perkins and the badly wounded Captain Murray.

Before he dies, Murray urges Sharpe to press on to Casa Antiga and

Richard Sharpe is just another sergeant in the 95th Rifles when luck and courage combine to change his fate forever. He saves the life of his commander and is made an officer

Major Blas Vivar and Comandante Teresa fight to free their country from the hated Napoleon, 'tyrant of Europe'

find Rothschild. He must also win over the men – particularly Harper. Murray gives Sharpe his own sword hoping it will inspire the men's trust.

But the Chosen Men will have none of it. They are lost in enemy territory, without a proper officer, and they want to go home. Led by Harper, they mutiny, and once more Sharpe must fight – this time for his life.

The fight is only stopped by the arrival of two of Wellesley's Spanish allies: Major Blas Vivar, and the beautiful partisan leader, Comandante Teresa, whose family were slaughtered by the French. Vivar explains that they are heading for Torrecastro, and offers to guide the Riflemen to Casa Antiga en route. Sharpe reluctantly agrees, and putting Harper under arrest, they go on together.

On the journey, Sharpe gets to know Teresa, though he doesn't discover the contents of the sealed chest she guards so jealously. As Murray advised, he applies himself to winning the men's trust, and little by little, they start to relax. Unbeknown to him, Hogan is keeping a weather eye on their progress from the hills.

They arrive at Casa Antiga to find it laid waste by the French. Sharpe and Teresa enter the village and after a short fight with some French cavalry, they discover a carriage bearing Mr and Mrs Parker, an elderly Methodist couple, and their daughter Louisa. But of Rothschild, there is no sign.

Returning for the unattended chest, they find Harper has untied himself and defended it - single-handedly - from two French cavalrymen led by a mysterious figure, the Man In Black. Having thus proved his loyalty, he is told by Sharpe to fall in. Harper joyfully obeys.

Although suspicious that his Spanish companions are not telling him all they know, Sharpe is growing increasingly attracted to Teresa. That night, they find comfort in each other's arms for the first time.

At dinner, Sharpe excuses himself and slips into the monastery to investigate the Spaniard's precious chest. But Teresa and Vivar prevent him. Instead, they explain: the chest contains a holy relic, the banner of the patron saint of Spain, which they plan to take to Torrescastro in order to inspire an uprising against the French - an uprising Sharpe is to lead.

Sharpe is outraged to find that he and his men have been used to support such superstitious nonsense and resolves to leave. But before he can do so, Hogan arrives and confirms Vivar's words: Sharpe is to escort Vivar to Torrecastro, take the town, and hold it long enough for the flag to be raised.

It is a grudging Richard Sharpe who agrees to carry on. But orders are orders, and though he cannot bring himself to forgive the Spaniards, he and the Chosen Men - including the newly-promoted Sergeant Harper, who now accepts that Sharpe as a proper officer - prepare the people of Torrecastro to take the town.

The battle for Torrecastro is fierce, but the Riflemen fight well and manage to repulse the French, led by Colonel de L'Eclin and the mysterious Man In Black. The other side come to parlay. The Man In Black turns out to be not only a Spanish collaborator working with the French, but the brother of Vivar. He claims to be fighting for a modern, progressive Spain, whereas his brother supports the Spain of yesterday. Sharpe refuses to surrender and the battle recommences.

In vicious hand to hand fighting, the Chosen Men take the tower and Vivar kills his brother at the steps of the altar. Amid cheering from the townspeople, the flag is raised, and for a few precious hours, the flame of Spanish resistance burns bright.

But not all the French are dead. As Sharpe helps Teresa onto her horse, she cries out a warning: Colonel de L'Eclin is riding down on Sharpe. The Rifleman draws his sword. 'No shooting,' he shouts. 'He's mine!'

The two men fight in the square and de L'Eclin appears to be getting the upper hand. He draws his pistol and a shot rings out. However, it is not Sharpe that falls but de L'Eclin. Sharpe angrily demands who is responsible, and young Perkins nervously owns up. Realising that the boy saved his life, Sharpe rewards him by making him a Chosen Man.

On returning to the British HQ, Sharpe finds Wellington well pleased with events at Torrescastro, but disappointed not to have recovered James Rothschild. Ah, but we did, says Sharpe, and with a flourish he takes the wig off Mrs Parker, revealing the laughing Rothschild beneath.

Sharpe and Teresa make love in a stable, and say their goodbyes. Finally, Sharpe is told by Hogan that his lieutenancy has been ratified by Horse Guards.

'SHARPE'S RIFLES' CAST

SHARPE	Sean Bean
HOGAN	Brian Cox
HARPER	Daragh O'Malley
TERESA	Assumpta Serna
WELLESLEY	David Troughton
VIVAR	Simon Andreu
COOPER	Michael Mears
HAGMAN	John Tams
HARRIS	Jason Salkey
TONGUE	Paul Trussell
PERKINS	Lyndon Davies
MAJOR DUNNETT	Julian Fellowes
CAPTAIN MURRAY	Tim Bentinck
SGT. WILLIAMS	Richard Ireson
LAWFORD	Martin Jacobs
COLONEL DE L'ECLIN	Malcolm Jamieson
MAN IN BLACK	Anthony Hyde
MR PARKER	Jack McKenzie
JAMES ROTHSCHILD	Kerry Shale
SCREENPLAY BY	Eoghan Harris

Sharpe's Eagle

SPAIN 1809.

SIR ARTHUR WELLESLEY, THE BRITISH COMMANDER, HAS CROSSED INTO SPAIN. NOW, TOGETHER WITH HIS SPANISH ALLIES, HE WILL DO BATTLE WITH THE FRENCH AT TALAVERA.

harpe is restive. Confined to bed with a serious leg wound, he and Harper - now comrades rather than enemies - watch as the pompous Colonel Sir Henry Simmerson arrives at the head of a new regiment, the South Essex. He is accompanied by his nephew Lt. Gibbons, a young hot-head named Lt. Berry, the veteran Major Lennox, and a cynical Virginian, Captain Leroy. Travelling with them is a beautiful young woman, the Countess Josefina, for whom Gibbons bears a passionate - and unrequited - love.

Though exhausted by their long march, the soldiers sparkle in absurdly clean uniforms and follow orders with parade-ground efficiency. But they look cowed and frightened, knowing they'll be flogged if they fail - as Simmerson demonstrates when one of the men faints with fatigue.

Wellesley is in his usual poor humour, and the arrival of the South Essex does nothing to improve it. He needs soldiers to fight this war, not flogged troops led by coffee house fops. But Wellesley knows

Sharpe fulfills a promise to the dying Major Lennox by taking a French eagle

Simmerson is not to be under-estimated: he and his friends have influence in London, and many are Wellesley's bitter opponents. To keep him sweet, Wellesley and Hogan decide to arrange a small military victory for him: he can go and blow up the bridge at Valdelacasa. Not certain that Simmerson is up to it, they give Sharpe the task of seeing that it happens.

Sharpe is none too pleased at the prospect of playing nursemaid to Simmerson and the South Essex but, lured by the prospect of promotion and the promise of seeing Teresa again, he agrees.

That night, Sharpe encounters Gibbons and Berry in the town. Mistaking Sharpe for a private, Gibbons demands his salute, and when it is refused, Berry raises his whip to strike him. Quick as a flash, Sharpe pulls Gibbons from his saddle and cocks his rifle at Berry. Only Hogan's swift intervention averts a duel.

The next day, Sharpe reports for duty. Simmerson is incensed by the realisation that the officer who is to accompany him is not 'a gentleman' - even more so when he hears it was Wellesley who raised him from the ranks. To spite Wellesley, he sets Sharpe the task of training the South Essex to fire three rounds a minute by nightfall. If he fails, they will be flogged.

It is only when he sees the South Essex at work that Sharpe realises the enormity of the task: these are amateurs. Harper looks on in grim amazement: 'Send 'em to Ireland,' he grunts. 'We'd be free in a week'.

But he and Sharpe bend to their task, showing the men by example, and teaching them methods that don't appear in any military textbook. When Simmerson arrives expecting victory, he is appalled to find that Sharpe has succeeded. It is a public humiliation Simmerson is unlikely to forgive.

That night, the regiment camps by the bridge at Valdelacasa. As usual, Berry and Gibbons play cards and, as usual, Gibbons loses heavily. Knowing that Josefina has no funds to pay her maids, Berry proposes they play cards for her. Whoever wins, he says, pays the maids: 'I'm sure the Countess will show her gratitude'. Gibbons agrees.

Berry wins, but when he goes to Josefina's tent to claim his prize, Sharpe comes to her rescue. Sharpe and Berry fight, and though Sharpe is outclassed, he has just enough strength to headbutt his opponent. Berry falls and immediately goes for his gun, but before he can fire, Hogan breaks up the fight. Sharpe formally takes the Countess under his protection. Berry seethes.

The next morning, Hogan begins mining the bridge. But before he can finish the job, Simmerson spots a small French patrol on the other side, and stupidly orders Major Lennox to chase it away. Lennox protests, but to no avail and Sharpe and Harper look on in horror as the men cross the bridge.

'This is a fool's mission,' mutters Lennox under his breath as he passes. 'Watch my flank, Sharpe.'

Sure enough, as soon as they are across, a horde of hidden French cavalry pour over the hill. The inexperienced redcoats panic, break formation, and try to run back across the bridge, while the French butcher them with ease.

Roaring his classic battle cry of 'Chosen Men!', Sharpe dashes across the bridge to their rescue, followed by the Rifles and – at the last moment – Captain Leroy. Simmerson panics and orders the bridge to be

blown up, leaving the stricken soldiers and their rescuers trapped on the French side. The French, their work complete, ride away, seizing the King's colours as they go.

Appalled by the loss of the Colours, Lennox's dying wish is that Sharpe avenge the insult by taking from the French an imperial eagle. Sharpe doesn't reply, but he implicitly accepts the task.

The following day, Wellesley demands an explanation. Simmerson's attempts to blame Lennox and Sharpe for the loss of the Colours are met with thundering rage. He has disgraced the entire army, says Wellesley, and to expunge the shame, he dismantles Simmerson's regiment, and gives command of the Light Company to the newly-gazetted Captain Sharpe. Simmerson storms out, vowing that Horse Guards will hear of this.

Wellesley congratulates Sharpe on his promotion to captain, but warns him not to jeopardise it with foolhardy heroics. He demands Sharpe's word that he hasn't promised to capture any eagles, and Sharpe replies – truthfully – that no one heard him make any such promise. Later, William Lawford – an old friend of Sharpe's from months spent together in an Indian prison – warns Sharpe to beware. If Simmerson can't damage Wellesley directly, he'll do so by having Sharpe – Wellesley's protégé – stripped of his commission.

Without money or political influence, the only way Sharpe can protect himself is by performing an act of such outstanding

The cowardly Sir Henry Simmerson loses the King's colours to the French, and blames Sharpe

valour that the army has to promote him. He must capture a French eagle at Talavera.

But Berry has other plans. He resolves to avenge Simmerson's humiliation. To do so, he and Gibbons visit Josefina and beat her cruelly. As they had intended, when Sharpe is told, he challenges Berry to a duel.

Duels are forbidden and mean certain demotion, but withdrawal means dishonour. The cunning Hogan saves Sharpe from either fate by sending him and Berry out on patrol together that night: given the chance, Sharpe will find his own way out of his predicament.

Immaculately uniformed and drilled to perfection, the South Essex are an imposing sight. But they have no battlefield experience. Will they stand, or will they run?

But it is Berry who makes the first move. Under cover of French fire, he shoots Sharpe in the leg and then follows him into the woods to finish the job. Suddenly a huge arm grabs him from behind. Harper, ever dependable, has sunk a knife into his ribs. Having relieved the dead man of his purse, Harper says a quick prayer and they leave the body behind the French lines and return to camp.

The Chosen Men mark the eve of battle with wild drinking, but Sharpe does not have the stomach for it. Instead, when Teresa arrives and tries to talk him out of any foolhardy plans to take an eagle, he demands fiercely whether she would care if he died in battle. She replies with equal fervour that she would.

The next day's battle at Talavera is huge and bloody. As expected, Simmerson turns tail and runs, leaving Sharpe to rally the South Essex. He does so, then, spotting his eagle, he leads the Chosen Men into a surprise attack on the French flank.

Step by step, the Chosen Men fight their way towards the eagle. Eventually Sharpe wrests it from the hand of a French soldier. Almost collapsing with fatigue, he drags it – and himself – back to camp, to push its tip into Lennox's grave as he had promised.

'SHARPE'S EAGLE' CAST

SHARPE	Sean Bean
HOGAN	Brian Cox
HARPER	Daragh O'Malley
TERESA	Assumpta Serna
SIR HENRY SIMMERSON	Michael Cochrane
WELLESLEY	David Troughton
LAWFORD	Martin Jacobs
JOSEFINA	Katia Caballero
COOPER	Michael Mears
HAGMAN	John Tams
HARRIS	Jason Salkey
TONGUE	Paul Trussell
PERKINS	Lyndon Davies
LEROY	Gavan O'Herlihy
LENNOX	David Ashton
GIBBONS	Neil Dudgeon
BERRY	Daniel Craig
DENNY	Nolan Hemmings
SCREENPLAY BY	Eoghan Harris

Sharpe's Company

SPAIN 1812. WELLINGTON BEGINS HIS INVASION OF SPAIN FROM PORTUGAL WHILST NAPOLEON IS PREOCCUPIED IN NORTHERN EUROPE. TO SUCCEED, HE MUST FIRST CAPTURE THE TWO GREAT FRONTIER FORTRESSES: IN THE SOUTH, BADAJOZ, AND IN THE NORTH, CIUDAD RODRIGO.

The siege of Ciudad Rodrigo is over, and victorious British troops are sacking the town in an orgy of looting and rape. Wellington plans his next objective – the siege of Badajoz – with his chief engineer, Fletcher, and his new spy master, Major Nairn.

Teresa and Sharpe snatch a few precious hours together. She tells him that she has had a baby. His joy at being a father becomes alarm when he learns that their baby daughter Antonia is in Badajoz. He vows to fetch her out.

A new draft of men arrives from England, accompanied by Col. Windham and Captain Rymer. Sharpe is appalled to discover that the sergeant in charge of the men is his old adversary, Obadiah Hakeswill.

A bullying, sadistic little man with an ugly facial twitch, Hakeswill's first act is to attempt to rape Teresa, whom he finds alone in a stable. Teresa is more than capable of defending herself, and it is only the arrival of Harper that stops her from killing him. Harper offers to finish the job, but Sharpe tells him that Obadiah Hakeswill is so evil that when he dies, it must be in front of his victims.

Sharpe warns Harper to watch Hakeswill's every move. He preys on soldiers. He blackmails them into giving him their money – and their wives – and protects himself by being servile to officers. Such is his guile that few officers see through him: it is only men from the ranks who can. It was Hakeswill's lies that got Sharpe flogged for a crime that he did not commit. Hakeswill, having once been hanged but not killed, believes himself to be immortal. His only weak spot is his affection for his dead mother, whom he talks to constantly.

After the incident in the stable, Hakeswill becomes obsessed with Teresa, determined to rape her as a way to hurt Sharpe. Col. Windham sends for Sharpe and tells him that the regiment now has more than its complement of captains, and Sharpe must give up his company.

Stunned, Sharpe, knows better than to protest. He is given a choice: be transferred as a captain, or stay on as a lieutenant. He chooses to stay and in a desperate bid for promotion, volunteers to lead the band of men who will go first into the breach at Badajoz. Of those who try, most will be killed – not without reason is this group called The Forlorn

Demoted to lieutenant and repeatedly denied command of the Forlorn Hope, Sharpe must fight for command of his company – and to free Teresa from the besieged city of Badajoz

Sharpe's feud with Hakeswill dates back to their days in India when Hakeswill had him flogged for a crime he did not commit

Hope – but any who survive can name their reward in money or rank. Sharpe knows that this is the only way he can secure a captaincy.

Leadership of the Hope is in Wellington's gift, not Windham's. For now, and to Hakeswill's delight, Sharpe is given the duties of a quartermaster. His noble Rifles are reduced to digging trenches for the siege.

Hakeswill takes every opportunity to belittle Sharpe's men, swapping their rifles for muskets, and taking away the green jackets they are so proud of. When Sharpe complains to Nairn that he and his men are soldiers, not clerks and trench diggers, he is told he can't swan around like a pirate for ever. Sharpe replies that Wellington will be glad of a few

pirates when he tries to take Badajoz. Again, he asks for command of the Hope. Once again, he is disappointed, Sharpe is too useful to throw away on a task like that; 'Wellington will kill you when it suits him'.

Meanwhile, the shells rain down from the French fort, and as fast as the British soldiers can dig the trenches, the French fill them in again.

Sharpe is summoned by Windham. The officer's baggage has been tampered with and a portrait of Windham's beloved wife is missing. The portrait's frame is found in Harper's bag, planted there by Hakeswill. Harper is brutally flogged and stripped of his rank.

Wellington's guns begin pounding the walls of Badajoz, and Sharpe

Badajoz, looking for women and loot, and Sharpe and Harper run to Teresa's house.

But Hakeswill has got there first. Having killed Teresa's father and Lt. Price, who had bravely tried to protect her, he has a dagger to Teresa's throat when Sharpe and Harper arrive. 'This your whore, Sharpie?' he sneers. 'Wanna watch?' Harper picks up Hakeswill's shako: 'This your mother, Obadiah?' Hakeswill howls, and when Sharpe spits into the hat he flings Teresa away and lunges at him. Sharpe punches him, and Hakeswill falls backwards over the banisters. The soldiers laugh as he struggles to his feet and stumbles out. Teresa rushes into Sharpe's arms. With tears of delight, he holds his child for the first time.

The next morning, Hakeswill has fled. Sharpe and Harper return to Windham the portrait of his wife, which Hakeswill had been keeping in his shako. Windham admits his mistake, apologises and immediately asks Harper for his forgiveness. He gives Sharpe command of the Light Company. Finally, Sharpe has a captaincy that cannot be taken from him.

'SHARPE'S COMPANY' CAST

SHARPE	Sean Bean
HARPER	Daragh O'Malley
WELLINGTON	Hugh Fraser
NAIRN	Michael Byrne
HAKESWILL	Pete Postlethwaite
TERESA	Assumpta Serna
WINDHAM	Clive Francis
FLETCHER	Nicholas Jones
COOPER	Michael Mears
HAGMAN	John Tams
HARRIS	Jason Salkey
PERKINS	Lyndon Davies
PRICE	Scott Cleverdon
COLLETT	Robert Morgan
SALLY CLAYTON	Louise Germaine
MRS. GRIMES	Soo Drouet
MATTHEWS	William Mannering
RYMER	Marc Warren
CLAYTON	Peter Gunn
DON MORENO	Peter Birrel
HOPE	Tat Whalley
BASED ON A SCREENPLAY BY	Charles Wood

fears that Teresa and their daughter will never come out alive. When the breach is finally made, Sharpe asks Wellington to allow him to lead the Forlorn Hope. He is refused, and – fearing for Teresa's safety – he asks Harper and his drink-sodden but good-hearted friend Lt. Price to swear to protect her if he cannot.

Darkness finds Sharpe guiding the leader of the Forlorn Hope, Captain Rymer, to the breach in the ramparts, then having to wait while they go forward. Others follow, and a bloody battle rages throughout the night. Hundreds die, and bodies litter the ground. When Sharpe discovers that Captain Rymer is among the dead, he at last takes his rightful place at the head of his men. Eventually, after hours of ferocious fighting, the British take the fort. Soldiers stream into the vanquished

Sharpe's Enemy

PORTUGAL 1813. WELLINGTON RESTS HIS ARMY BEFORE RESUMING HIS OFFENSIVE AGAINST NAPOLEON. BUT IN THE NO MAN'S LAND BETWEEN THE TWO ARMIES, OTHER FORCES ARE STILL ACTIVE.

A motley bunch of deserters – French and Portuguese, as well as British – have taken the Spanish village of Adrados. Led by the irascible Marshal Pot Au Feu and Obadiah Hakeswill, they have taken prisoner two English women, Sarah Dubreton and Lady Isabella Farthingdale.

In Wellington's camp, Sharpe is inspecting new weapons: the rockets of Lt. Gilliand's division. However, the rockets are loud but hopelessly inaccurate, and Sharpe warns Gilliand that unless he improves their aim, the rocket division will lose its horses to soldiers who can make better use of them. Meanwhile Sir Augustus Farthingdale has arrived with 500 guineas for his wife's ransom. A coward, a snob and a stickler for good manners, when he hears it is Captain Sharpe of the 95th Rifles – a rogue from the ranks – who is to recover his wife, he makes no secret of his disgust.

Sharpe and Harper are accompanied to Adrados by Teresa and the Chosen Men, but the last few miles they must go alone. Watched from a balcony by the deserters and their captives, they enter the convent and warily scout the cloisters before being suddenly confronted by two French officers doing the same thing. Both take the others for deserters, and they fight fiercely, only calling a halt when Sharpe sees they carry gold and realises that they are both on the same mission. In fact, one of the French officers is Sarah Dubreton's husband. Sharpe calls to the

unseen kidnappers to come and get the gold. As soon as Hakeswill steps forward, Sharpe recognises his old enemy, and it is with difficulty that Pot Au Feu maintains calm. Sharpe, Harper and Dubreton are taken inside to inspect the captives. Asked how she fares, Sarah responds with a quotation from a poem: though her husband recognises that it's a coded message, he cannot decipher it.

Hakeswill informs the rescuers that he has upped the price. They have five days to bring the extra money or the women will be raped. To make his point, he orders Sarah to be stripped. To save Sarah's blushes, Lady Farthingdale insists on taking her place. She opens her bodice, and Hakeswill insists that Sharpe take a good look. 'My compliments, ma'am,' says Sharpe politely. As they leave, Sharpe asks Dubreton if he intends to mount a rescue. He replies that he would die for his wife, but that because she is English, he has been forbidden by Major Ducos, the French spy master, to risk French lives in the attempt.

Back at camp, Lord Augustus is furious not to have his wife back. But armed with Sharpe's information, Nairn realises that Ducos is planning an invasion of Portugal from Adrados – a far more dangerous situation than was at first envisaged. He decides to thwart Ducos' plan by

Having infiltrated the rebel camp by night, Sharpe and the Chosen Men launch a surprise attack at dawn

The beautiful Lady Isabella Farthingdale is held hostage by Hakeswill's band of rapacious rebels: can Sharpe save her?

Harper attacks Hakeswill, but the rebels hold all the cards

capturing the town first with a detachment of rifles. But first, Sharpe must go in to secure the women's safety.

Sharpe, promoted to major, inspects the new detachment, the 60th Rifles, and is appalled at their untidiness. Their captain, William Frederickson, looks worse than any of them, but when Sharpe reprimands the men for being dirty, Frederickson replies 'Men are dirty, sir. Rifles are clean.' Sharpe calls for a shooting demonstration, and Frederickson's men prove their worth.

Reassured, Sharpe sets off for Adrados that night. His men overpower the guard at the gate and creep in, only to be met by Kelly, one of the British deserters. However, Sharpe recognises him as a former Connaught Ranger who distinguished himself at Talavera, and asks him if he wants to join them. Relieved, Kelly does so. Cooper picks the locks of the women's cells. Sharpe posts sentries outside, and spends the night in Lady Farthingdale's room where they renew an old friendship from the days when she had been a common prostitute, and he her client.

At the appointed hour the next morning, the Chosen Men launch their attack on the unsuspecting deserters, throwing explosives from the balcony into their midst as they sleep. Outside the gates, Frederickson is waiting, and when the deserters attempt to flee, they are met with volley after volley from his Rifles.

An almighty battle ensues, and when it is over, Sharpe kneels by the dying Kelly. 'Clean slate, sir?' asks the boy. Pressing the coveted chevron into his hand, Sharpe says 'Chosen Man, Kelly'. But there is no time for mourning. Hakeswill has fled, and he has Isabella over his saddle.

As luck would have it, he rides straight into Teresa, who is coming to warn Sharpe of the French invasion. Hakeswill shoots her in cold blood. Too late, Dubreton arrives. He arrests Hakeswill and escorts the dying Teresa back to Adrados on a horse-drawn cart. Broken-hearted, Sharpe

kneels beside her and kisses her for the last time. Ducos arrives and gives them one hour in which to surrender. Sharpe refuses and says they have horse, foot and artillery and will fight. He calmly helps Sarah onto her husband's horse and repeats that he has horse, foot and artillery: he will fight to the death. Nairn, knowing he does not, is nonplussed.

Teresa is buried with full honours. Ducos urges an attack but the French commander, General Chaumier, has too few men to risk it. It is only when Ducos gives him a signed statement saying the British have no cavalry that Chaumier agrees to attack. Spotting the rocket men and taking them for cavalry, the French retreat in disarray. The rockets are fired – successfully, for once – and the French break and run. A pall of smoke lies over the dead. On a nearby hill, Sharpe and the Rifles watch and cheer. Chaumier looks grimly at Ducos and holds up the worthless piece of paper.

Hakeswill is taken back to face a firing squad, and this time, he does not escape. The grief-stricken Sharpe goes in search of Antonia, picks her up and holds her close.

'SHARPE'S ENEMY' CAST

SHARPE	Sean Bean
HARPER	Daragh O'Malley
WELLINGTON	Hugh Fraser
NAIRN	Michael Byrne
HAKESWILL	Pete Postlethwaite
TERESA	Assumpta Serna
SIR AUGUSTUS	Jeremy Child
LADY FARTHINGDALE	Elizabeth Hurley
SARAH DUBRETON	Helena Michell
POT AU FEU	Tony Haygarth
COOPER	Michael Mears
HAGMAN	John Tams
HARRIS	Jason Salkey
PERKINS	Lyndon Davies
FREDERICKSON	Philip Whitchurch
DUCOS	Feodor Atkine
DUBRETON	Francois Guetary
GILLIAND	Nicholas Rowe
CHAUMIER	Vincent Grass
RAMONA	Diana Perez
KELLY	Morgan Jones
SCREENPLAY BY	Eoghan Harris

Sharpe's Honour

1813. WELLINGTON HAS BEGUN HIS

GREAT OFFENSIVE TO FINALLY DRIVE THE FRENCH FROM

SPAIN. NAPOLEON, DEFEATED IN RUSSIA, HIS ARMIES IN NORTHERN

EUROPE IN RETREAT AND DISARRAY, IS DETERMINED TO

HOLD SPAIN AT ALL COSTS.

I n the French camp, Napoleon is contemplating a proposal by Major Ducos. For the price of one death and one imprisonment, Britain will leave Spain with no more shots being fired. The deposed Spanish King Ferdinand will end his alliance with Britain, sign a treaty with France, order Britain to leave Spain and then the French will withdraw. All it needs is the assurances of the Spanish nobility, her generals and – most importantly – the church, that they will accept.

In the British camp, Sharpe sits alone by the fire, mourning Teresa. Harper and his woman, Ramona, heavily pregnant, watch him sadly. He needs a good battle, says Harper. He needs a good woman, she replies.

In an office inside a French garrison in Spain, Ducos is arguing with a wealthy, beautiful woman – La Marquesa Helene Mendora – whose carriages he has impounded. Although they work on the same side, it is clear that there is little love lost between them. Ducos berates her for being half English, being married to a Spaniard, and yet working for the French. I fight for France, replies La Marquesa. You fight for yourself, sneers Ducos. In exchange for the return of her property, she must write a letter to her husband saying she's left him because a British officer forced his attentions on her. The officer's name is Richard Sharpe.

In the British camp, the outraged Marques sends his second to Sharpe to demand an apology or a duel. Knowing he has never even met La Marquesa, Sharpe refuses to apologise, and the duel goes ahead.

After a hard fight, Sharpe has his sword to the Marques's throat when Major Nairn rides up. Duels are strictly forbidden, and Nairn insists the fight is passed off as friendly sword practice.

But there are limits even to Nairn's influence, and when the Marques is murdered in his bed that night, and witnesses are found to testify that Sharpe was in the vicinity at the time, Nairn cannot save him. The Spanish demand retribution, and to protect his relations with his allies, Wellington agrees to a court martial. Sharpe is found guilty, stripped of his rank and condemned to death. Wellington himself attends the execution. Sharpe is dead.

The following day the real assassin – a bullet-headed Spanish partisan known as El Matarife – and his brother the Inquisitor, Father Hacha, meet Ducos in secret. Ducos orders them to obtain letters from the Spanish nobility assuring the king that peace with France is

Unjustly accused of murdering a Spanish officer, Sharpe is sentenced to hang. Wellington signs the death warrant

Sharpe extricates his accuser, La Marquesa, from a convent where she has been an unwilling nun; they head back to camp

acceptable. He also wants them to make La Marquesa enter a convent so that he can claim her wealth.

They carry out their tasks, and while Father Hacha terrorises the Spanish nobles into writing letters supporting an alliance with France, El Matarife ambushes La Marquesa's carriage and unceremoniously dumps her at a convent.

That night, without explanation, Nairn takes Harper on a mission. They ride for miles before Nairn stops to ask Harper if he believes in ghosts. Harper looks at him oddly. 'Here's a ghost for you, Sgt. Harper', says Nairn: out of the darkness walks Sharpe.

Nairn explains that Ducos is trying to drive a wedge between the British and their Spanish allies. By falsely accusing Sharpe of insulting a Spanish officer, he had hoped to deepen the rift. But Sharpe has been saved for an important task: he must capture La Marquesa so Nairn can discover Ducos' next move. Sharpe and Harper set off. Evading capture by El Matarife's partisans, they eventually find La Marquesa in a convent. Despite the protests of the nuns, they get her out and make their escape.

The three fugitives are on the run for several hours, during which time the mutual dislike between Sharpe and the woman who tried to

destroy him is replaced by a strong attraction. But they cannot escape. Luckily for La Marquesa, the French find them before the Spanish do. They allow her to go, but Sharpe is captured and taken back to Santa Maria for questioning by Ducos.

Harper alone escapes. He makes his way back to camp. Ignoring Nairn's protests, he collects the Chosen Men and – after a glimpse of his new-born son – sets off to rescue Sharpe. The men are perplexed: surely Sharpe was hanged? 'You know the army, boys,' replies Harper. 'They couldn't hang a curtain.'

In Santa Maria, Sharpe is interrogated by Ducos. Refusing to answer Ducos' questions about La Marquesa, he is viciously beaten and his precious telescope – given to him by Wellington in thanks for saving his life – is systematically smashed. 'An eye for an eye, Sharpe', he says viciously. It is a foolish gesture. While Ducos talks, Sharpe inches his way towards the broken telescope, uses a piece to cut his bonds, and sets about fighting back. Alarmed, Ducos shoots and then runs.

Meanwhile, the Chosen Men have ambushed some French soldiers, put on their uniforms, and blagged their way into Santa Maria. Hearing the shot, they storm the cell, grab Sharpe and escape. Harris sets alight a barrel of gunpowder as he goes, triggering a huge explosion.

The men arrive at Wellington's side just as the battle of Vitoria is about to begin. Sharpe reports to Wellington that Ducos is trying to engineer a treaty with King Ferdinand to drive the British out of Spain, and Wellington – well pleased – tells Sharpe to resume his command.

Sharpe rallies the men and the French are on the run. Even Ducos, stumbling through the battlefield after the fighting is over, is shot by his own soldiers.

After the battle, Sharpe spots El Matarife riding off with La Marquesa across his saddle. He shouts a challenge and El Matarife stops, hurls La Marquesa to the ground, and throws down his fighting chain. The two men lunge at each other, but Sharpe prevails, eventually forcing El Matarife to admit that he and his brother work for the French. Appalled at this betrayal, one of El Matarife's own men shoots him.

Afterwards, La Marquesa comes to thank Sharpe with a gift – a new telescope. They bid one another a passionate farewell.

'SHARPE'S HONOUR' CAST

SHARPE	*Sean Bean*
HARPER	*Daragh O'Malley*
WELLINGTON	*Hugh Fraser*
NAIRN	*Michael Byrne*
LA MARQUESA	*Alice Krige*
DUCOS	*Feodor Atkine*
FATHER HACHA	*Nickolas Grace*
COOPER	*Michael Mears*
HAGMAN	*John Tams*
HARRIS	*Jason Salkey*
PERKINS	*Lyndon Davies*
NAPOLEON	*Ron Cook*
EL MATARIFE	*Matthew Scurfield*
RAMONA	*Diana Perez*
MENDORA	*Ricardo Velez*
VERIGNY	*Jay Benedict*
VAUGHAN	*James Saxon*
MOTHER SUPERIOR	*Anna Savva*
PAKENHAM	*Mark Burns*
REV WHISTLER	*Christopher Own*
FATHER SANCHEZ	*Ricardo Montez*
SCREENPLAY BY	*Colin MacDonald*

The partisan leader El Matarife turns out to be a collaborator working for Ducos and the French. Although a fearsome fighter, he finally meets his match in Richard Sharpe

Sharpe's Gold

SUMMER 1813. WELLINGTON'S ARMY

IS DRIVING THE FRENCH OUT OF SPAIN. BEFORE THEY CAN REACH

THE PROTECTION OF NAPOLEON'S MARSHAL SOULT, FRENCH WAGON

TRAINS COME UNDER RELENTLESS ATTACK.

aving watched the last few French soldiers flee after a battle, Sharpe is gunning for a different foe. He's after the British infantry who failed to cut off the French retreat. When he finds their leader, Sgt. Rodd, he discovers why: he and his men are deserting.

Lt. Ayres and his provosts arrive too late to catch them. Instead, Ayres arrests Rifleman Skillicorn, Sharpe's newest recruit, for stealing a wild chicken. Fiercely protective of his men – even good-for-nothings like Skillicorn – Sharpe forces Ayres to release him at the point of a gun.

It is a foolish act, and one for which Wellington's chief spy, Munro insists Sharpe must make a humiliating public apology. Even so, Ayres hangs Skillicorn. From that day forward, he and Sharpe are at war.

They soon have another reason to be enemies when Ellie Nugent, a pretty young Irishwoman, arrives in camp. A relative of Wellington's, she and her mother Bess are in Spain to find Ellie's father, lost while searching for a hoard of Aztec gold buried in the hills nearby. However,

Young Ellie Nugent defends Lt. Ayres during a French attack
– and Sharpe makes sure the provost doesn't forget it

Wellington refuses to mount a search party, and orders the women to return home the following day.

At a dinner before they go, a drunken Lt. Ayres challenges Ellie to prove her rumoured skill with a rifle against Sharpe. Ayres bets heavily on Ellie, and for nine rounds, she and Sharpe are neck and neck. Then Sharpe gallantly fires a blank and forfeits the contest. But Ellie sees his action and insists he re-fires. It's a bull's eye. She throws her arms around him, and Ayres silently concedes the loss of both the wager and the girl.

Meanwhile, Wellington has weightier concerns. Desperately short of men for the advance into France, when a Spanish partisan named El Casco offers to exchange 52 captured British deserters for Baker rifles, Wellington agrees. Sharpe is instructed to manage the exchange and – to his disgust – will be accompanied by Ayres, whose men will guard the deserters on their return journey.

Before they leave, Ayres attempts a reconciliation: after all, he says, they will be the only two officers on the expedition. But for Sharpe, rank is no guarantee of integrity, and he vents his anger with a punch. Ayres meekly accepts his punishment and a fragile truce is agreed.

When Sharpe and the Chosen Men have saved Ellie's father from El Casco's slaughter house, they discover a mass of gold.

Believing it to be tainted by El Casco's cannibalistic rituals, they blow up the entire cave system in which it is hidden

After travelling a few miles, the men realise they are being followed. It is Bess and Ellie, who claim they have Wellington's permission to join the expedition. Although Sharpe isn't fooled, he can hardly send them back alone. In these mountains – El Casco's mountains – he senses the presence of evil all around him.

Almost immediately, they encounter some French soldiers. Once again, Ellie proves her skill with a rifle, shooting one who tries to kill Ayres, but later, horrified at having taken a life, she breaks down in tears. When Sharpe tries to comfort her, their long-delayed physical contact unleashes an explosive passion and they make love.

The men are joined by Munro, and as they march, Ayres adds to the growing sense of unease with stories that the local people are descendants of the Mexican Aztecs and engage in human sacrifice.

At the rendezvous, El Casco inspects a sample rifle and orders them to return in two days. He rides off, throwing down a captured French dispatch as he goes. It contains plans for a French counter offensive by Marshal Soult – crucial information – and Munro sets off to inform Wellington immediately.

On the appointed day, Sharpe hands over the rifles in exchange for 52 deserters, and a small bag of treasure. One of the deserters is smoking a pipe which Ellie recognises as her father's but, unable to persuade Sharpe to look for him, she and her mother slip away to carry on alone.

Exasperated by the risk they are taking, Sharpe sends the provosts back with the captives, and goes after them. Ayres is intent on proving his manhood, and volunteers to join him.

The search party comes across a group of French cavalry, and after a battle, finds the diary of their leader, Jean Luc Barbier, which confirms that the locals do indeed carry out human sacrifices. It reveals that Barbier had been on a mission to destroy the pagans, and their leader - none other than El Casco.

Meanwhile, Bess and Ellie are ambushed by a group of Spanish guerrillas. Bess is killed and Ellie carried off to a mountain hideaway. Barbier is hidden in a nearby thicket, and he watches horrified as El Casco's men flay one of his soldiers alive before bringing in their next victim: Ellie.

Barbier runs. When he finds Sharpe, he gives himself up and explains in broken English what he has seen. Sharpe's party head for the caves.

Ellie is thrown into a cave to await her fate. Surrounded by carvings of the vengeful gods that guard her prison, she sees a man huddled in the corner: her father. But relief soon turns to despair. Nugent is clearly unhinged. He is gibbering the names of Aztec gods, and shows

no reaction to news of his wife's death. Some of El Casco's women come in and begin preparing Ellie for sacrifice. Drugged and dizzy, she watches as El Casco advances on her with a ceremonial knife.

Outside, Sharpe devises a plan. On his signal, Barbier and Rifleman Harris shout orders to two non-existent companies of French infantry, drawing the guerrillas away from the caves. This gives Sharpe and Harper – joined by Ayres – time to find Ellie.

Ayres is killed as he enters the cave, but Sharpe attacks El Casco, who fights hard before escaping into the maze of caves. Sharpe follows, cornering his adversary in a cavern gleaming with a hoard of treasure. The two men fight, and Harper arrives to shoot El Casco and save Sharpe's life.

Afterwards, Sharpe has his men blow up the cave, treasure and all. Pausing only to pay their respects at the place where Bess was killed, they return to camp, where Sharpe gives Wellington El Casco's small bag of loot. 'Is that all there was?' asks Munro. 'Yes, sir,' replies Sharpe. 'That's all.'

'SHARPE'S GOLD' CAST

SHARPE	Sean Bean
HARPER	Daragh O'Malley
WELLINGTON	Hugh Fraser
HAGMAN	John Tams
COOPER	Michael Mears
HARRIS	Jason Salkey
PERKINS	Lyndon Davies
MUNGO MUNRO	Hugh Ross
BESS NUGENT	Rosaleen Linehan
ELLIE NUGENT	Jayne Ashbourne
WILL NUGENT	Peter Eyre
EL CASCO	Abel Folk
PROVOST MARSHALL	Philp McGough
AYRES	Ian Shaw
BARBIER	Julian Sims
RAMONA	Diana Perez
SKILLICORN	Philip Dowd
RODD	Peter-Hugo Daley
TRIPPER	Nicholas McGaughey
DONKIN	Jake Abraham
SCREENPLAY BY	Nigel Kneale

Sharpe's Battle

SEPTEMBER 1813. WELLINGTON IS

CHASING NAPOLEON BACK THROUGH THE PYRENNEES INTO FRANCE.

A FINAL VICTORY SEEMS CLOSE AT HAND, BUT THE FRENCH ARE

FIGHTING A FIERCE REAR-GUARD ACTION AND EACH YARD OF GROUND

GAINED IS PAID FOR IN BRITISH BLOOD.

Lost in the Spanish hills, Sharpe's men come across a desecrated English wagon train and the remains of the town of Casa Antiga, both sacked by the soldiers of the fearsome French commander, Brigadier General Guy Loup. One of the officers shouts for Sharpe and then is violently sick. Harper goes to investigate the cause of his distress and finds the bloodied body of a young baby. What animals would do such a thing? Harris, who speaks a modicum of Spanish, is dispatched to find out which unit the invading troops were from. He returns with information that they're of the Wolf Brigade, named after Brig Gen Guy Loup, their commander, who is know for maintaining the loyalty of the local Spanish to the occupying French by endless blood-letting. 'Well,' says Sharpe. 'We all know what to do with wolves.'

Perkins rescues a young woman from rape by two of Loup's soldiers and they are put under arrest. When Loup arrives, demanding their release, Sharpe defiantly calls for a firing squad and has them executed in front of him. Loup vows revenge.

Meanwhile Wellington and Munro are debating what to do with King Ferdinand VII of Spain's gift of the Royal Irish Company – his palace guard. Having little use for such green men, Wellington posts them next to the French lines and appoints Major Sharpe to knock them into shape. The sooner they desert, the sooner he's rid of them.

Already the worse for one encounter with Sharpe, their colonel, Lord Kiely, is doubly enraged to find Sharpe inspecting the Irish Company without permission.

But Sharpe has been given his orders. Slowly and painfully, he teaches the Irish to fight, winning respect as a hard-bitten battlefield soldier rather than a parade-ground swordsman like Kiely. But it's hard work – for both Sharpe and the soldiers – and as a result of the loss of the wagon train, they are perilously short of ammunition. As predicted, the desertions begin.

Hopelessly idealistic about war, Kiely indulges in a showy sword fight with two French cavalrymen in pursuit of a Spanish partisan, Dona Juanita de Elia, who is riding to join the Irish Company. The men are impressed. Sharpe, however, is not.

Sharpe's men go into Loup's town to retrieve the much-needed ammunition. They are attacked and Kiely, too proud to retreat, has to be almost dragged away. They lose 17 men.

Nearby are the bodies of the deserters, butchered by Loup. Sharpe tells the Irish soldiers they have three choices – go east and be slaughtered by the French, go west and get shot for deserting, or stay here and learn to be soldiers. They choose to stay.

But even Sharpe has difficulty preventing a mutiny when the men hear reports of an English massacre back in Ireland. Harper himself mutters gloomily that the ghost of Cromwell has come to drench Ireland in blood, and Sharpe has to appeal to friendship over nationalism to maintain his loyalty.

Sharpe's gallantry has even won over Lord Kiely, and he is favoured with an invitation to dinner at which he witnesses the revolting display of Kiely fawning over Dona Juanita and snubbing his wife. Later, Sharpe learns that ever since Lady Kiely had a miscarriage, her husband has been gratifying his sexual appetites elsewhere – currently with Dona Juanita. That night, Lady Kiely comes to Sharpe's tent, begging him to end her husband's affair and offering herself in return. Sharpe declines her offer, but agrees to speak to Lord Kiely.

But Loup is an altogether tougher adversary, and Sharpe knows that Wellington is resigned to losing the Irish Company if necessary. Determined not to die without a fight, Sharpe uses every available man and weapon in defence of their position. Every available woman too: even Ramona, Miranda – the woman Perkins rescued at Casa Antiga – and Lady Kiely are given pistols.

Only Dona Juanita exempts herself from the work, returning from a ride in the hills to report that there is no threat from Loup from that quarter. Sharpe doesn't believe her.

A surprise night attack by Loup proves him right. There is a fearsome battle and the Irish Company succeed in fighting him off. Sharpe wants to press their advantage with an immediate counter-attack, and Juanita promises the support of her partisans – a dubious gesture, since no-one has ever laid eyes on any of them.

Lady Kiely chooses this moment to reveal that she is pregnant. With sudden concern for her well-being, her husband sends her home to safety and promises to give up Juanita. But Lady Kiely's coachman O'Rourke is in the pay of the French, and delivers her to Loup. Miranda sees Juanita meet Loup, but before she can warn Sharpe, Juanita has her killed.

She dies in vain: that night, Juanita reveals her true identity to Kiely, warning him that unless he keeps the Irish Company out of the battle, his wife will die.

When Sharpe's men go into the town, they find it well defended – somehow, Loup has been warned. Sure enough, a flood of French soldiers pours from every house, and soon they are fighting for their lives. When Sharpe fights his way back to Kiely to find out why the Irish

are not with him, Kiely says they're surrendering. Furious, Sharpe draws his sword and challenges him to a duel. Juanita steps forward to shoot Sharpe, but Kiely's honour can take no more. He kills her and confesses to the men that she was a spy. Sharpe appeals to them not to let Loup make fools of them, and they stream into battle.

Back in the town, the Rifles are fighting a losing battle. In a desperate move, they fake death to finish off a group of French soldiers. It works, but in a cruel irony, Perkins is mortally wounded by the turncoat O'Rourke. He dies in Harper's arms. The enraged Irish sergeant goes after his killer, and savagely stabs him – once for Perkins, once for Ireland, and once for himself.

Meanwhile, Kiely has found his wife's prison, but before he can free her, Loup runs him through with a sword. Sharpe arrives and they duel. Initially, Loup seems to be winning, but after an exhausting battle, Sharpe prevails and his opponent dies with the cheers of the Irish Company ringing in his ears. Beaten by a mere palace guard.

Sharpe reports to Wellington, making special mention of the bravery of Kiely and Perkins. Later, he rebukes Munro for failing to warn him that Juanita was *afrancesado*.

He and Lady Kiely bid each other farewell, and the Chosen Men fire a sad salute over the grave of their fallen comrade, Perkins, and his lass, Miranda.'

'SHARPE'S BATTLE' CAST

SHARPE	*Sean Bean*
HARPER	*Daragh O'Malley*
WELLINGTON	*Hugh Fraser*
MUNGO MUNRO	*Hugh Ross*
HAGMAN	*John Tams*
HARRIS	*Jason Salkey*
PERKINS	*Lyndon Davies*
LORD KIELY	*Jason Durr*
LADY KIELY	*Allie Byrne*
RUNCIMAN	*Ian McNeice*
LOUP	*Oliver Cotton*
JUANITA	*Siri Neal*
O'ROURKE	*Liam Carney*
RAMONA	*Diana Perez*
MIRANDA	*Maria Petrucci*
SCREENPLAY BY	*Russell Lewis*

Under Sharpe's tutelage, the untried Irish
Company rout the more experienced French force

Sharpe's Sword

The Franco-Spanish frontier, 1813. The French army is retreating from Spain, but Napoleon is planning a surprise counter-attack. To succeed he must first flush out and capture Wellington's master spy - El Mirador.

A carriage travelling through the Spanish countryside is ambushed. Its occupants are tortured and killed, and only a terrified young nun escapes.

Later, the French soldiers responsible for the ambush are themselves attacked by the English. The French colonel shoots his own captain and then puts on his jacket as a disguise. He then hides his code book before surrendering to Sharpe. He claims his name is Captain Dumas and that his colonel was killed in the attack by the English.

Something about him makes Sharpe suspicious. The man claims to trade horses, yet he carries a Kliegenthal, the best sword ever made. In his pockets are papers covered in figures, which he says are bills of sale, but which could be codes. But before Sharpe can test him further, Col. Berkeley of the South Essex arrives. Using Captain Lord Jack Spears as an interpreter, he accepts the man's parole.

Moments later, the terrified young girl emerges from hiding and

When Sharpe discovers that his friend Jack Spears is working for the French, Father Curtis - alias 'El Mirador' - advises Sharpe that 'Men are seldom as they seem'

throws herself on Sharpe's mercy. He calms her as best he can, and takes her back to be cared for by Ramona. But the trauma of the attack has left her speechless, and whenever he has to leave her, she clings to him and sobs piteously. They christen her 'Lass'.

Meanwhile, Munro summons Sharpe and tells him that Napoleon has sent a French colonel to capture and interrogate a British agent named El Mirador. Although Munro is unable to divulge the identity of El Mirador, he instructs Sharpe to go to Villafranca to find and kill the colonel. Sharpe asks if Dumas' dead colonel could have been Leroux. Munro thinks not.

Back in the tents, Ramona and Harper are bristling at one another. Ramona wants to get married but Harper, though he loves her, will not. When asked why, he says it would hurt his mother. Sharpe tells him to get on with it.

Still sceptical of Dumas' story, Sharpe requests a court of honour in which to question him. Col. Berkeley presides, and Jack Spears is appointed the defendant's advocate. Sharpe shows that Dumas fits the colonel's tunic and not the captain's, and argues that the man is Leroux and should be put under guard until Major Munro's return. Berkeley demurs and Dumas remains on parole.

Back in his tent, Sharpe examines a fragment of Voltaire's *Candide*, which Harris found when they captured Dumas. Suspecting it to be a code book, they resolve to find another copy in a library in the town.

At Villafranca the South Essex is met by Sharpe's old enemy, Sir Henry Simmerson, who is in charge of the town. Just as Simmerson is pompously declaring the French fort to be no threat, there is a loud bang and a cannon ball lands in their midst. In the confusion, the prisoner escapes, proving Sharpe right – he is Leroux.

Sharpe meets Father Curtis, the fierce Irish priest who runs the hospital. At dinner, Father Curtis agrees to persuade Harper to marriage. In exchange, Sharpe must return Lass to the church.

The South Essex storm the fort and Sharpe confronts the French spy. But before he can kill Leroux, a French officer drags him to safety. The South Essex is repelled, and as they fall back, Sharpe is hit by a bullet and gets lost in the fray.

Harper, Ramona and Lass search for him among the injured, eventually finding him in the room reserved for those beyond hope.

Sharpe is discovered unconscious and with an infected stomach wound: but Ramona and Lass refuse to let him die

Father Curtis examines his wounds and confirms the diagnosis. A serious cut to the left shoulder and an infected bullet wound in his stomach. He'll be dead by dawn.

Harper reluctantly obeys Father Curtis' injunction to leave Sharpe to the care of Lass. Instead, he begs a sword from Father Curtis' collection from which to forge a replacement for the one which Sharpe broke at the fort. In payment, he agrees to marry Ramona.

Harris finally finds the book he needs and sets to work on the code, while Lass operates on Sharpe to remove the bullet and stitch his wound. She goes to Mass for the first time since her ordeal, and later, when Simmerson tries to have his way with her, she has him looking down the barrel of his own gun before throwing him out and returning to Sharpe's side.

Though the surgery worked, Sharpe's fever is dangerously high. Father Curtis decrees kill-or-cure: he prescribes ice-cold water to break the fever. The Chosen Men go to work with buckets.

Lass wakes next morning to find Sharpe up and about – weak but on the mend. She speaks his name, they kiss, and then make love.

Afterwards, Harper, Harris and Hagman welcome Sharpe back from the dead with the new sword and the deciphered French message, signed by Jack Spears. Seeing Sharpe's distress, Father Curtis – who Sharpe now knows to be El Mirador – commiserates over the dilemma he faces.

Alone in the library, Spears tells Sharpe he was blackmailed into becoming a spy by Leroux. But he is not without principles. It was not money he wanted, but because the honour of a lady was at stake. Spears had refused to kill Father Curtis when he discovered his identity, and he denies betraying Col. Berkeley, saying to do so would have meant betraying Sharpe.

Sharpe is faced with a difficult choice. An officer would have Spears court-martialled and let his family die of shame. A gentleman would give him a pistol and let him blow his brains out. Instead, Sharpe offers him the chance to lead the South Essex into glory the following day, and Spears accepts. They both know it means certain death.

The South Essex are lined up and waiting. At a signal from Sharpe, Spears rides ahead to plant the flag as far into enemy territory as possible. Though hit again and again, he limps forward, flag in hand,

Once his real allegiance is discovered, Spears' fate rests in Sharpe's hands

until the French hack him to death. The South Essex falls silent. Then it charges forward as one.

Sharpe runs too, limping on his injured leg. There is a violent battle, culminating in Harris and Hagman throwing lighted tapers into the French weapons store. Again, Sharpe's men have won the day.

Sharpe agrees parole for all the officers except Leroux, whom he takes on in single combat. Sharpe fights with one arm clamped across his stomach wound, and Leroux with a leg injury sustained in their previous encounter. When Leroux finally succumbs, Sharpe himself collapses, only to be dragged to his feet by Hagman. Harper is dying. He must come quickly.

Father Curtis is bending over Harper, asking for any last requests. Harper wishes he'd married Ramona. A rapid wedding ceremony later, he is told to get up and kiss the bride. 'I thought you said I was going to die, Father' says the astonished Harper. Father Curtis laughs back, 'Sure, we're all going to die, Patrick.'

'SHARPE'S SWORD' CAST

SHARPE	Sean Bean
HARPER	Daragh O'Malley
HAGMAN	John Tams
HARRIS	Jason Salkey
LASS	Emily Mortimer
LEROUX	Patrick Fierry
SPEARS	James Purefoy
BERKELEY	Stephen Moore
MUNGO MUNRO	Hugh Ross
SIR HENRY SIMMERSON	Michael Cochrane
FATHER CURTIS	John Kavanagh
DON FELIPE	Vernon Dobtcheff
RAMONA	Diana Perez
CONNELLY	Pat Laffan
FATHER O'SULLIVAN	Walter McMonagle
ENSIGN MCDONALD	Matthew Pannell
SCREENPLAY BY	Eoghan Harris

Sharpe's Regiment

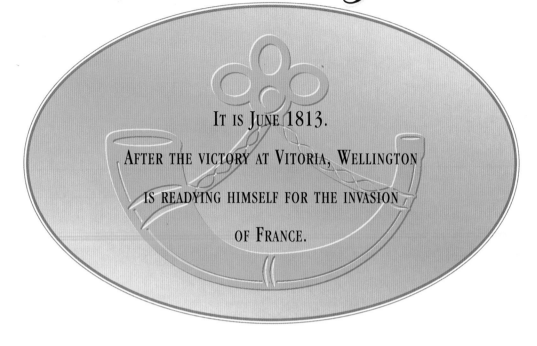

IT IS JUNE 1813.

AFTER THE VICTORY AT VITORIA, WELLINGTON

IS READYING HIMSELF FOR THE INVASION

OF FRANCE.

The depleted South Essex is a battalion at half strength. Wellington's chief intelligence officer, Major Ross, receives a letter from Lord Fenner, Secretary of State at War, informing him that the Second Battalion has been reduced to a holding battalion and the regiment is to be disbanded. Smelling a rat, Ross sends Sharpe back to England to find replacements and save the regiment.

Sharpe and the newly promoted Sergeant Major Harper arrive at Horse Guards to learn that there are 700 men waiting for them in Chelmsford, but when they go there, they find the barracks all but deserted. They find less than a dozen men – a drummer, two teenage boys, a veteran soldier with a wooden leg and a few more – but of the others, there is no trace.

Sharpe learns nothing from Captain Carline, the officer of the day. However, Sgt. Ted Carew, a veteran of Talavera, shows him ledgers which prove the Battalion is still recruiting, but says he hasn't seen a new recruit for months.

Sharpe's enquiries are interrupted by a summons to attend the Prince Regent court. Deeply uncomfortable among the frippery and finery of high society, Sharpe is made to tell the Prince Regent how he captured the French eagle at the battle at Talavera. By dinner time, Prinny is re-telling Sharpe's story as if he himself were there.

Seizing his chance, Sharpe tells Prinny of his missing regiment. But when the prince demands an explanation of Lord Fenner, he is stonewalled. The Second Battalion marches only on paper, he is told, this is a bureaucratic matter, part of the province of Prinny's brother, the Duke of York. Fenner glares menacingly at Sharpe, and Sharpe knows he is defeated.

As Sharpe leaves, Fenner quietly details Lady Anne Carmoynes, his mistress, to find out what he's after. She spirits Sharpe off to bed. Later, she warns him not to trust Lord Fenner, then, refusing to say more, she dismisses him.

Sharpe visits Maggie Joyce, an old friend from his days in the Rookery, and after a drunken evening together she agrees to find a buyer for his soldier's booty. He is leaving her gin palace when he is attacked. It's Harper, come to warn him he's being followed. When two men leap out of the shadows, Sharpe and Harper kill them. To their shock, one of the thugs is in the uniform of the South Essex. Sharpe has Maggie spread the rumour that he and Harper were killed, and they go

Simmerson and his fellow conspirators hunt runaway recruits for sport: on this occasion the quarry is Pat Harper

*Despite the splendour of Court, Sharpe realises Prinny is an enthusiastic
but essentially powerless admirer*

undercover and enlist.

Recruiting officer Sgt. Horatio Havercamp is a swaggering, self-important little man, who promises men the earth to get them to enlist, and then takes away from them what little they have. Along with two young boys named Marriott and Charlie, Sharpe and Harper join up.

Havercamp's good humour evaporates overnight, and he marches the new recruits to a training camp far from Chelmsford, where he turns them over to the savage Sgt. Lynch and Lt. Col. Girdwood. Both men hate and fear soldiers – particularly Irish ones – and put them through a merciless drill.

Sharpe and Harper keep their noses clean and their eyes open.

Before long they realise that Girdwood is training up men to be auctioned to other regiments. Before he can take cover, Sharpe encounters Sir Henry Simmerson's niece Jane. Sharpe has loved her from afar since they once met years before, and he can't help looking at her. She is equally pleased to see him, and when he explains his mission, she confirms his suspicions. He resolves to go to Horse Guards with the news, and she agrees to steal money and provisions and leave them in the boathouse for his journey.

When he gets back to the men, Sharpe finds the lovesick young Marriott has deserted. The officers mount a man hunt, chasing the unfortunate Marriott into the sea. Sharpe dives in to rescue him, but the boy is cold-bloodedly shot by Lynch.

Incensed by this cruelty, Harper sets on Lynch, and before he knows what has happened, the hunt is on again, but this time Harper is the quarry. Sharpe overcomes his guard, steals a horse and rides to Harper's aid. After a heart-stopping chase, the two men make for the boathouse and escape.

Once again they go to Horse Guards, where Sharpe tells his old friend Lawford, now a politician, of the conspiracy. Lawford says he'll take care of it, but, hoping to avert a scandal, he takes the information straight to Fenner.

Lady Anne overhears Fenner's conversation with Lawford, and goes to the Rose Tavern to warn Sharpe. She says they must join forces to find proof of the conspiracy and ruin Fenner. When asked why, she relates that he had destroyed her husband and has used her as a whore ever since.

The next day, Sharpe bursts into Girdwood's chambers, bluffing that he has orders from the Duke of York himself. He puts Girdwood under arrest and orders Carline to search for the ledgers that will furnish him with the proof he needs. Meanwhile, Harper takes over the parade ground, and avenges himself on the terrified Lynch.

Unable to find the evidence he seeks, Sharpe lets Girdwood escape so that he can lead him to the ledgers. He follows Girdwood to Simmerson's house where Jane is in fear of her life. She tells him that Simmerson beats her and is forcing her to marry Girdwood. Sharpe enlists her help, hoping he can protect her after the present problems are resolved: although frightened, she agrees to go to London to get him the ledgers.

Sharpe takes his new battalion on a night march to London to meet the Prince of Wales – thereby hoping to force Fenner to acknowledge their existence. En route, they stop to collect arms from Chelmsford and buy white chickens, whose feathers Sharpe mysteriously saves. Then they press on to the Theatre Royal, where Prinny and the court are to attend a re-enactment of the Battle of Talavera.

At the height of the re-enactment, Sharpe's men burst into the display, slashing their way through the painted backdrop and – in full view of the entire court – pledge their allegiance to Prinny. To the prince's delight, they place his emblem – three white feathers – behind their shako plates, and he renames them the Prince of Wales' Own Volunteers.

The next day, Sharpe presents his case to Gen. Sir Barston Maxwell at Horse Guards. But without evidence to back up his claims, Fenner can afford to ignore him. He says the battalion is being sent to Spain under Girdwood, and Sharpe will be sent to Australia.

Then the tables are turned. Lady Anne barges in and produces one of the ledgers, having hidden the other one out of Fenner's reach. She threatens to expose the scandal, forcing Fenner to concede that the battalion will go with Sharpe to Spain. Sharpe has won.

As he and Anne walk out into the sunshine, Sharpe sees Jane in Simmerson's carriage. He helps her from the carriage and – by way of offering protection from her uncle – proposes marriage. She hesitates and then accepts.

Back in Spain, the men follow Sharpe gladly into battle, striking fear into the hearts of the French. Harper gleefully puts Girdwood and Lynch through hell, and young Charlie manages to shoot a French officer. Finally Sharpe's regiment sets foot on French soil.

'SHARPE'S REGIMENT' CAST

SHARPE	Sean Bean
HARPER	Daragh O'Malley
JANE GIBBONS	Abigail Cruttenden
SIR HENRY SIMMERSON	Michael Cochrane
FENNER	Nicholas Farrell
LADY ANNE CAMOYNES	Caroline Langrishe
ROSS	James Laurenson
LT. COL. GIRDWOOD	Mark Lambert
PRINCE REGENT	Julian Fellowes
HORATIO HAVERCAMP	Norman Rossington
HAGMAN	John Tams
HARRIS	Jason Salkey
CHARLIE WELLER	Steve Chambers
MARRIOTT	Henry Woolley
SGT. LYNCH	Robert Patterson
MAGGIE	Julie T. Wallace
LAWFORD	Benedict Taylor
SMITH	Tristram Wymark
CAPT. CARLINE	Adam James
ROSSENDALE	Alexander Armstrong
SGT. CAREW	Peter Jonfield
YOKEL	Simon Smith
SIR BARSTAN MAXWELL	John Savident
MRS GREY	Diana Payan
DOCTOR	David Batley

Sharpe's Siege

WINTER 1813. WELLINGTON IS GATHERING HIS FORCES READY FOR THE FINAL PUSH TO PARIS. NAPOLEON HAS DISPATCHED HIS BEST AGENT, MAJOR DUCOS, AND THE FORMIDABLE PEASANT-GENERAL CALVET, VETERAN OF THE RUSSIAN CAMPAIGN, TO FIND OUT WHERE THE INVASION WILL BEGIN.

t Wellington's HQ, the debonair Compte de Maquerre, a pro-Bourbon Frenchman working for the British, argues that Bordeaux is ripe for rebellion. Wellington's doughty spy master, Major General Ross, is doubtful.

To test the idea, he suggests using Maquerre's own castle, 60 miles behind French lines, as a base from which to foment revolt. Maquerre reluctantly agrees, pointing out that since his mother and sister turned the castle over to Napoleon, it must first be captured.

However, unbeknown to Maquerre, Wellington's real objective is to use an assault on the castle to keep General Calvet busy, freeing Wellington's own men for the more important task of attacking Marshal Soult's forces. He appoints a new colonel, Horace Bampfylde, to lead the attack, with Sharpe in support.

For Sharpe, seeing command of his battalion go to an arrogant, inexperienced young firebrand is a bitter pill.

Under the doubtful leadership of Col. Horace Bampfylde, the Redcoats are unable to take Maquerre's castle from the French

He consoles himself with the thought of his impending marriage to Jane. However, during the ceremony, Ross collapses with fever and soon afterwards, Jane who has made daily visits to his sickbed, develops the same symptoms. Sharpe sends for the doctor.

Dr Kenefick confirms that the prognosis is bad for both patients. He has reserved for himself a small supply of quinine, the only known cure for yellow fever. Sharpe leaves, knowing that his wife and his dear friend Ross have little chance of recovery.

He is accompanied, though he doesn't yet know it, by another loyal friend: Harper. Despite explicit orders to the contrary, and though technically surplus to requirements, Harper is unable to see Sharpe go on a mission without him. So he secretes himself in a cart, nursing a raging toothache and injured pride, and waits for the right moment to reveal his presence.

On reaching their destination, Bampfylde, thirsty for glory, sends Sharpe, Frederickson and the Rifles on a scouting mission so that he can take the castle alone. He fails, and is forced to retreat with heavy casualties. Maquerre has no difficulty persuading him to forget the fort and concentrate on the task of raising the rebellion.

But Bampfylde has reckoned without Sharpe. Seeing the carnage from afar, Sharpe resolves on a more subtle approach. He, Frederickson and Harris disguise themselves as allies of the French and ask for medical attention for a wounded comrade. The comrade in question is Harper, smeared with the blood from the newly-extracted tooth. Once inside the castle, they quickly force the French to surrender.

Sharpe lets the soldiers go, but allows Lucille, Maquerre's sister, to remain behind to nurse her mother who, like Jane, has the fever.

Bampfylde returns and, shamed by Sharpe's victory, sends him off on a reccé. Sharpe's departure is watched with interest by Maquerre, now back with his real comrades, the French. Maquerre sees this as an opportunity to dupe Bampfylde into vacating the castle and, disguising Ducos as the mayor of Arcon, he returns to Bampfylde bearing false news that the region is ready to change sides, Calvet is on his way and Sharpe is dead.

The cowardly Bampfylde is persuaded that his mission is accomplished. He sets off for Wellington's camp to tell of his own

For the Redcoats, Sharpe's bravery and determination are in stark contrast to the cowardice of the young Colonel Bampfylde

bravery, destroying the fort's defences before he goes and heartlessly leaving the wounded behind to fend for themselves.

Meanwhile, Sharpe and his men have ambushed a French convoy, and captured its small but precious store of quinine. His conversations with local people reveal that the region is far from ready to rise up against Napoleon, and confirm his suspicions that Maquerre is a double agent.

Returning to the fort, Sharpe learns that his old enemy Ducos is about to bring the full force of Calvet's army down upon his defenceless castle. He is faced with a difficult choice: escape now, have Bampfylde court-martialled and live to fight another day, or stay to face Calvet and certain death. He stays.

Despite the fact that he is her enemy, Lucille begs Sharpe for a share of the quinine for her mother. He refuses, determined to conserve it to save Jane's life. But later he relents. He has accepted reality: he has no hope of getting out of the castle alive to deliver it.

Lucille repays his kindness by telling him the cellar is full of oyster shells from which he can make a defensive weapon: lime to blind the French attackers. That night she comes to his room offering to pay the balance of her debt with her body. Sharpe declines her offer, and she leaves embarrassed.

Maquerre, confident of victory, comes to the fort under a flag of parley to discuss the British surrender. The Rifles refuse their terms and even Lucille – more surprised than Sharpe to see her brother in the uniform of the French imperial guard – finds herself unable to forgive him for lying to the family for 15 years. She too will stay in the fort.

Maquerre returns to his troops and the attack begins. Calvet sends his first column directly towards the broken gates. Desperately short of ammunition, Sharpe limits his men to five shots apiece, targeting the officers and NCOs to create maximum disorder in the French ranks. When the remainder of the soldiers are close, he signals for the lime to be thrown. Soon the French conscripts are howling with pain, throwing down their muskets and clawing at their eyes.

They burst through the open gates to be confronted by four ranks of riflemen. Each man has ammunition for ten volleys only, after which they're bluffing.

With Harper and Harris pitching oil and burning bales of hay onto the French from above, those who aren't shot are burnt to death.

Just before the Rifles exhaust their supply of ammunition, the French turn and run. The second column needs no further telling. It too turns and flees.

Sharpe knows this is but a temporary respite: he cannot withstand a second attack.

However, at the crucial moment, Calvet receives news that the entire fort incident was a British ruse to keep him from aiding Soult. Realising that his military career could be over, he vents his rage on Ducos.

Inside the fort, Sharpe has received the same news. He returns to camp in time to correct Bampfylde's distorted report of events and see him arrested and stripped of his rank.

To his delight, Jane is in the hospital – but as a nurse, not a patient – and Ross too is recovering well. Sharpe and Jane are reunited, each with a new-found respect for the other's achievements.

'SHARPE'S SIEGE' CAST

SHARPE	Sean Bean
HARPER	Daragh O'Malley
JANE GIBBONS	Abigail Cruttenden
WELLINGTON	Hugh Fraser
ROSS	James Laurenson
DUCOS	Féodor Atkine
MAQUERRE	Christian Brendel
BAMPFYLDE	Christopher Villiers
CATHERINE	Amira Casar
FREDERICKSON	Philip Whitchurch
PALMER	James Ryland
CALVET	Olivier Pierre
ROBINSON	Danny Cunningham
HAGMAN	John Tams
HARRIS	Jason Salkey
KENEFICK	John Tordoff
SMITHERS	Jim McManus
REILLY	JD Kelleher
BRIGITTE	Nicola Murray
FYTCH	Nick Mollo
SCREENPLAY BY	Eoghan Harris

Sharpe's Mission

FRANCE 1813. THE STRUGGLE
BETWEEN FRANCE AND BRITAIN IS ENTERING ITS FINAL STAGES.
THE DUKE OF WELLINGTON HAS TAKEN ONE STEP OVER THE
PYRENEES. NAPOLEON NEEDS TO KNOW WHERE HE WILL
TAKE HIS SECOND.

T wo hardy French veterans – Colonel Cresson and General Calvet – join forces to plan the capture of Wellington's head of intelligence, Major General Ross.

Back in the British camp, while Harper, Harris and Hagman compete for the attentions of a flirtatious gypsy named Conchita, Sharpe is enjoying the pleasures of married life. Jane, however, is looking to the future. Bored with wars and armies, she is eager for the excitement of civilian life as an officer's wife. At the same time, however, she is anxious about how Sharpe will take to a life of parties, dinners and dancing.

But Sharpe has not yet outgrown his usefulness to Wellington. Colonel Brand, a bold but wayward British officer who operates behind French lines, plans to destroy Calvet's main powder supply in the Rocha cave system. Wellington orders Sharpe to act as back up.

Though disappointed not to be in command himself, Sharpe has seen Brand's bravery under fire in a previous encounter, and he is pleased to be working with him again. He is less than delighted, however, that they will be accompanied by an insipid young war correspondent-cum-poet named Shellington. Also in the party will be an explosives expert called Major Septimus Pyecroft. A strange, solitary figure, Pyecroft usually works alone between French and English lines and is regarded as one of Wellington's bravest and most skilful

technicians. However, because of an accident that left his face badly mutilated, he wears a hood and is rarely seen in public. The accident was the fault of Ross, and there is palpable hostility between the two.

As Wellington and Ross already suspect, Brand is not what he seems. He secretly meets with the French to fine-tune a plan to capture Ross. When Brand realises he has been spotted by two elderly gypsies, he has them killed. Unbeknown to him, their daughter Zara escapes the blood bath. Pyecroft finds her desperately trying to bury the bodies, and the doughty old warrior takes pity on her and silently buries them himself. He then takes her to Wellington's camp and the protection of a band of gypsy camp-followers. Despite his deformity, Zara recognises his great compassion, and a strong attraction develops between them.

Brand arrives in camp to hold a briefing for his fellow officers. He will travel to Rocha a day ahead of the main party, and he persuades Ross to accompany Sharpe to gather intelligence. Although Ross and Wellington suspect Brand's loyalty, they do not reveal their suspicions. Once again, Sharpe will be left to deal with the problem.

Zara sees Brand arrive, recognising her family's horses among his, she knows her parents' murderer is among his men. She tells Pyecroft, hoping for a time when she can get revenge, and Pyecroft tells Sharpe.

Jane is not so perceptive. She invites Brand and Shellington to

Sharpe and Major General Ross go in search of Septimus Pyecroft, the explosives expert with a grudge

dinner, and while she plays the society hostess and Brand the conquering hero, Shellington fawns over them both. Sharpe is withdrawn and surly throughout.

Meanwhile, Harper too is having marital problems. His boyish infatuation with Conchita has angered Ramona, and to get her own back, she has indulged herself in a mild flirtation with Pope, one of Brand's men. Things get out of hand, Pope and Harper fight, and for once, Harper comes off worst.

Of her three admirers, Conchita decides upon Harris, but when he arrives at her tent that night, he finds her and her family dead. He reports the murders, only to find himself regarded by the provost as a suspect, and confined to camp. Sharpe arrives, and from Brand's comments, realises he must have been involved. Keeping his suspicions to himself, Sharpe gives Harris the task of looking after Jane in his absence, and readies himself for the expedition.

Meanwhile, Cresson asks Calvet for a compliant group of French

deserters. He sets up some of them as an easy target for 'Brand's Boys' so that they can reinforce their reputation as heroic French-slayers. The others he sends to Rocha, to form a weak guard which he knows will fall easily when the time comes for Brand to capture it.

Shellington quickly tires of war, and fakes an illness so that he can return to camp and the lovely Jane. Sharpe sees the chance to trap Brand, and summons him to arrange an escort for Shellington. At the same time, he lets Brand know that Zara, the witness to his crime that he thought he had silenced, is still alive, and will spend the night alone with Pyecroft. And then he waits.

When Brand's loyal sergeant, Pope, goes to kill Zara, he is captured. Sharpe, Harper and Hagman round up Brand, his co-conspirator Crake and their men. Pyecroft uses his explosives techniques to get a confession out of Pope.

Pope admits that he and Brand murder and spy for the French. Rocha is intended as bait for Ross: the French were to capture him, and

Brand's Boys would take the fort from the soft soldiers and return to Wellington with at least a partial victory. Pope reveals that Brand has been faking his daring exploits against the French for years – and mocks Sharpe for being taken in by him.

Sharpe marches the men to Rocha where he persuades the timorous French to surrender. He then sets about defending the fort against Cresson just long enough to blow the powder store and escape.

Cresson arrives and battle begins. Recognising that the British are unlikely to prevail, Sharpe determines on another objective: to bring Brand to justice. He calls for a court martial and Brand is found guilty. But realising that Horse Guards will let him off the hook, Sharpe executes his own form of justice by throwing him down the well.

Sharpe offers Crake a chance to die honourably by forming a rear guard to enable the others to escape. Crake accepts, and Sharpe and his party slip through the caves to safety. When Pyecroft's explosives go up, Calvet feels the blast 50 miles away, and with characteristic decisiveness,

has Cresson shot for failing to carry out Napoleon's orders.

Sharpe returns home to a faithful wife. Shellington's attempt to woo her with risqué poems had been thwarted by Harris, who recognised them as the work of others. Jane had come to her senses just in time, and when Sharpe asks Harris for his report, the rifleman is able to report nothing more serious than a small skirmish.

Having routed Col. Brand and destroyed the French powder supply in the Rocha caves, the 95th is ready to press on into France. Sharpe, Harper, Hagman and Harris will march again

Riding one-handed, and with Zara mounted behind him, Pyecroft still manages to scatter bombs for his French pursuers

'SHARPE'S MISSION' CAST

SHARPE	*Sean Bean*
HARPER	*Daragh O'Malley*
JANE GIBBONS	*Abigail Cruttenden*
ROSS	*James Laurenson*
WELLINGTON	*Hugh Fraser*
BRAND	*Mark Strong*
POPE	*Andrew Schofield*
PYECROFT	*Nigel Betts*
PERCY SHELLINGTON	*Warren Saire*
HAGMAN	*John Tams*
HARRIS	*Jason Salkey*
RAMONA	*Diana Perez*
CRESSON	*Peter Le Campion*
CALVET	*Olivier Pierre*
CRAKE	*Christian Rodska*
ZARA	*Berrín Polítí*
PROVOST MARSHAL	*Michael Mallinson*
CONCHITA	*Aysun Metíner*
SCREENPLAY BY	*Eoghan Harris*

Sharpe's Revenge

APRIL 1814. TOULOUSE IS ONE OF THE LAST
FRENCH TOWNS STILL HOLDING OUT AGAINST THE BRITISH.
FOR NAPOLEON, LOSING IT MEANS HE MUST ABDICATE
AND MAKE WAY FOR KING LOUIS.

In the half light of dawn, General Calvet paces back and forth among his sleeping soldiers. Nearby, Colonel Maillot and Major Ducos watch as Napoleon's personal fortune is loaded onto a cart. If Calvet loses Toulouse, Ducos and Maillot must spirit the treasure away to safety before the Bourbons – or the British – can steal it.

In Sharpe's bedroom, Jane wakes to find her husband writing a note giving her power of attorney over all his money. Suddenly fearful, she makes him promise that this will be his last battle and that, when it is over, he will return with her to England. If he breaks his promise, she swears she will return without him. Sharpe agrees.

Later, Sharpe joins his men, and watches the first British brigade under Colonel Wigram beaten back by the French. As Wigram stumbles back to the line, blaming his men for the rout, Sharpe replies that it is a bad workman who blames his tools. Then he goes to work.

Sharpe and his riflemen move smoothly up the slope to Calvet's fort, dispatching a rank of French infantrymen, and sweeping onwards. Behind them follow the stalwart Captain Frederickson and Major General Ross, with their respective troops.

At home, waiting anxiously for her husband's safe return, Jane is visited by her friend, Lady Spindacre. Young, shrewd and penniless, Molly Spindacre is keenly aware that all that stands between herself and the poorhouse is a rather tawdry affair with Colonel Wigram. She hears Jane's account of having been given power of attorney by Sharpe, and instantly sizes up the situation.

Meanwhile, out on the battlefield, the British are gaining ground. When Sharpe's men breach the battlements, Calvet realises that all is lost. He tells Ducos to take Napoleon's treasure to safety. Before doing so, Ducos sees Sharpe stagger and fall. Anxious to settle an old score, he attacks Sharpe with his sword. But Sharpe fights him off, and as the beaten Frenchman scrabbles piteously for his glasses, sends him crawling back to Calvet on his hands and knees.

The victorious Redcoats swarm over the fort, and Ross invites his officers to dinner to celebrate. But Wigram is still smarting from his own humiliation. He insults Sharpe and a duel is arranged.

Frederickson cheerfully elects himself Sharpe's second and takes his man off to drink to the fall of Napoleon. Both glad the war is over, they dream of a quiet life at home – particularly Frederickson, who envies Sharpe both his marital bliss and his fortune.

Ducos and his men set off with the treasure. To test their loyalty, Ducos idly asks them if they have considered stealing it. Maillot's shocked denial proves his constancy, but Challon admits that he has. Ducos sees his chance to steal Napoleon's treasure, and make it appear

Jane Sharpe longs to return to England: when she does so, she falls for the charming but sly Lord Rossendale

that the crime is Sharpe's.

That night, he orders Maillot to return to Toulouse and report that their precious cargo has been stolen by Sharpe. When Maillot refuses, Ducos dismisses him and sends him home to Normandy. Ducos and Challon shoot those of the remaining soldiers who are not in league with them. Then Ducos mutilates the bodies, saying sardonically to Challon as he does so, 'Major Sharpe is a monster, isn't he?'

At dawn the next day, Molly finds Jane distraught. Sharpe has not returned and Jane believes him dead. Molly cruelly tells her that he soon will be – he has challenged Wigram to a duel. Furious that Sharpe has broken his promise not to fight again, and keen to punish him, Jane agrees to Molly's suggestion that she return to England without him.

Molly, of course, undertakes to go too.

The duel is a tense affair. Wigram fires first, misses, and then gibbers with fear as Sharpe takes his time to line up his shot. At the crucial moment, Ross arrives with news of Napoleon's abdication. Sharpe moves his pistol down Wigram's body, and calmly puts a bullet through his opponent's buttock.

When Sharpe learns that Jane plans to go to England without him, he rides after her, leaving Wigram writhing on the ground, as much from the wound to his pride as the injury to his rear end.

Sharpe arrives home to find Jane gone and the provosts waiting to arrest him. To his surprise, this is not for fighting an illegal duel, but on suspicion of stealing Napoleon's treasure and murdering two of its

Sharpe's loyal friend Frederickson champions his cause in a duel and a military tribunal, but loses out to him in love

114

guards. He is ordered to appear at a tribunal the following day to decide whether he should be court-martialled. Stunned, Sharpe asks who will preside over the tribunal. The answer fills him with dread: 'Colonel Wigram'.

The next day, M. Roland, who represents the new French administration, tells the court that the treasure was under the care of Col. Maillot but, after the fall of Toulouse, it was placed in the care of one Major Ducos.

Shocked to hear Ducos' name, Sharpe allows Frederickson to conduct his defence. Frederickson calmly challenges a sworn deposition from Maillot claiming that Sharpe led the attack. Why is its author not here to give evidence, he asks. Frederickson demands that the evidence must be better than this if it is to put Sharpe on trial for murder. He calls for habeas corpus – the prosecution must present the body. Wigram grudgingly concedes, and Roland undertakes to bring Maillot from Normandy to give evidence. Until then, Sharpe must stay in jail.

In London, a charming young officer Lord Rossendale arrives at Jane's house with news of Sharpe's arrest. Jane faints, and Molly has Rossendale carry her to bed. In a trice, Rossendale is smitten.

Also hearing of the tribunal, Ducos realises his mistake. He sets off for Normandy with the treasure, determined to kill Maillot before Roland finds him and hears the real story. Sharpe, too, languishing in jail, has realised that Maillot is crucial to his defence. He, Harper and Frederickson escape, and while Harper goes to London bearing a letter of apology from Sharpe to Jane, the others make for Normandy.

Now hiding out in the hills, Calvet learns of Sharpe's escape. Convinced that the fugitive will go to retrieve his booty, which he guesses is by now hidden in Paris, he sends Gaston after him.

Meanwhile, Maillot, still in uniform, sits at the breakfast table of his sister Lucille, struggling with his conscience. He tells her he should have reported Ducos to their superiors. Lucille tries to convince him that this is all in the past, and eventually Maillot agrees. After all, he says, Sharpe's the killer. Sharpe's the thief.

Before he can explain, Maillot hears the arrival of strangers. Hiding his sister in the house, he seizes his pistol and goes outside. But the visitors shoot him dead. All that Lucille hears as the murderers run off is the name 'Major Sharpe'.

Not surprisingly, therefore, when Sharpe and Frederickson arrive at the Maillot farm, they are met by Lucille and a blunderbuss loaded with nails. When Sharpe introduces himself, she shoots him.

Back in London, hearing that Sharpe has escaped, and will inevitably be hunted down and shot, Jane turns to Rossendale for con-

Thinking he had murdered her brother, Lucille tries to kill Sharpe; she later discovers the truth, and they fall in love.

solation. He is infatuated with her beauty and wealth, and uses his persuasive powers to seduce her.

Sharpe is more restrained. Over the next few weeks, while Frederickson nurses him back to health, Sharpe falls deeply in love with Lucille. Remembering his marriage vows, however, he resists the urge to make love to her. He is even honourable enough, on learning that Frederickson is also smitten, to commend his friend to Lucille.

Lucille knows Frederickson's feelings, and although unable to reciprocate them, she treats him with compassion. One evening, she

When Sharpe's tribunal re-convenes, Lucille gives evidence on his behalf. Her testimony — and Calvet's sworn statement — confirm his innocence. France drops its charges against him and makes a full apology

observes that he does not wear the spectacles she once found in his pocket. He says they are not his but Ducos'. Lucille is shocked to hear once again the name that her brother had spoken just before his murder, and Frederickson explains his suspicions that it was Ducos who murdered Maillot and made it look like Sharpe's work. But where is he now? Lucille suggests asking the maker of the spectacles, M. Juliot of

Paris, and Frederickson sets off immediately.

Meanwhile, Harper reaches London and tries to speak to Jane, but she refuses to see him. That night, he breaks into her room and leaves Sharpe's message. From then on, Jane's conscience knows no peace.

When Frederickson finds M. Juliot, he also discovers Ducos' whereabouts — he has holed up in a well-defended villa in Naples. But

Frederickson is himself discovered by Gaston and Calvet, who insist he takes them to Sharpe and the treasure.

Frederickson manages to convince them that it is Ducos, not Sharpe, who has the treasure. Calvet realises that he has been double-crossed, and resolves to hunt down Ducos in Naples. But first, he and Frederickson must return to the Maillot farm to get Sharpe.

Lucille and Sharpe are now living in harmony, though their passion remains unconsummated. She tells him that the war is over, and he is free to go home to his wife. But Sharpe disagrees. Until his innocence is proven, he tells her, he has no home. The intensity of their longing for each other is becoming dangerous. Unwilling to trust himself, he goes out to sleep in the barn.

There he finds Harper, newly returned from London. Sharpe asks for Jane's reply to his letter and realises from Harper's embarrassed response that he has lost her love forever. He returns to the house.

Sharpe and Lucille wake together the next morning to the sound of a French wedding song, sung by the newly-arrived Calvet and his guardsmen. The lovers join in the good-natured laughter, though Sharpe is painfully aware that his friend Frederickson is deeply hurt to find Lucille in Sharpe's arms. That morning, Sharpe and his new French allies plan their journey to Naples to take back the treasure from Ducos. Calvet, a general, demands command of the expedition, but Sharpe insists that it's a skirmisher's job. Frederickson bristles at Sharpe throughout. They set off for Naples, with Frederickson still furious at Sharpe's perceived betrayal.

In London, Jane summons Molly and tells her Sharpe is free and she fears reprisals. Since all Sharpe's money is now invested in Rossendale's various schemes, she asks to borrow some to escape. Molly refuses. Now that Jane has no disposable income, she is no longer useful. Molly drops her and takes herself back to France and Wigram.

Having thought that he and his stolen treasure would be safe in Naples, Ducos is terrified when he finds that Sharpe and Calvet have traced him there. Leaving Challon to defend the villa with a small portable cannon and a handful of men, Ducos goes in search of re-inforcements.

Sharpe and his men silently climb the slope to Ducos' fortified villa, unseen in their green uniforms. After a vicious battle with the defenders, they enter his castle, quickly followed by Calvet. Challon dies defending his treasure, but Ducos is nowhere to be found.

But not for long. Ducos returns with a hundred men. From outside, he shouts insults at Sharpe, but promises him a clean death – and Calvet safe passage out – if they surrender themselves and the gold. Sharpe is given two minutes to decide his fate.

Sharpe hits on the idea of loading the cannon with pieces of gold. He has Frederickson fire these over the heads of the soldiers below. Sure enough, as the men hear the clink of gold falling on the rocks, they break ranks and run to collect what they can. Struggling to maintain control, Ducos breaks cover – and Sharpe shoots him.

While Frederickson keeps the enemy soldiers busy by raining gold on their heads, Calvet and his men pass the rest of Napoleon's treasure to their comrades outside and carry it away to their waiting boats.

After the battle is over Sharpe returns to Toulouse to face his accusers. Wigram restarts the tribunal, expecting to send Sharpe to a court martial. But Roland stops him in his tracks. Reading a sworn statement from Calvet about Ducos' deception, and with Lucille on hand to give evidence, Roland recounts the story of what really happened. Soon France is dropping its charges against Sharpe and making a full apology.

Wigram is obliged to find there is no case to answer. Sharpe says farewell to Frederickson and they part friends. And to Lucille, he says *au revoir*, and pledges to return.

'SHARPE'S REVENGE' CAST

SHARPE	Sean Bean
HARPER	Daragh O'Malley
JANE	Abigail Cruttenden
LUCILLE	Cecile Paoli
FREDERICKSON	Philip Whitchurch
CALVET	John Benfield
DUCOS	Feodor Atkine
ROSSENDALE	Alexis Denisof
COLONEL MAILLOT	Stephane Cornicard
SGT. CHALLON	Phil Smeeton
ROSS	James Laurenson
WIGRAM	Tom Hodgkins
LADY MOLLY SPINDACRE	Connie Hyde
HOPKINSON	Milton Johns
ROLAND	Paul Brooke
SALMON	Michael Fitzgerald
JULIOT	Leon Lissek
GASTON	Ercument Balakoglu
SCREENPLAY BY	Eoghan Harris

Sharpe's Justice

SUMMER 1814. PEACE.

NAPOLEON HAS BEEN EXILED TO THE

ISLAND OF ELBA. THE KING OF FRANCE HAS BEEN

RETURNED TO HIS THRONE. AND SHARPE

HAS COME HOME TO ENGLAND.

The war is over and Sharpe has returned to England. Bereft of friends at Horse Guards, and estranged from his wife Jane, Sharpe accepts a posting in Scarsdale, Yorkshire, the town where he grew up. He is to head a private militia raised by a mill-owner named Sir Willoughby Parfitt, and his task is to protect Parfitt's mills from a rebellious and restless workforce. Harper insists on going along too, not displeased at the prospect of breaking a few English heads.

In Scarsdale, some mill workers gather to listen to a man named Truman speak. The war is over, he tells them, but what does the long-awaited peace mean for them? Nothing more than a lot of ex-soldiers coming and taking their jobs.

Back in London, Jane is finding life as Lord Rossendale's mistress problematic. Although she loves Rossendale, London society disapproves of her liaison and refuses her entry. This is made painfully clear when she and Rossendale meet Lady Anne Camoynes, an old flame of Sharpe's, in the park. Lady Anne asks Rossendale barbed questions about Sharpe. Jane is pointedly ignored.

Sharpe and Harper reach Yorkshire and are met by the local yeomanry, under the command of the insolent young Captain Wickham. The

yeomanry offer them an escort to Shireburn Hall, where they are expected by Sharpe's new master. As they ride, Harper notices that they are being followed. They give chase and Sharpe shoots one of their pursuers and corners another. The second man escapes, but not before Sharpe recognises him as Matt Truman, a lad he grew up with in the workhouse in nearby Keighley.

Sharpe arrives at Shireburn Hall and finds Parfitt brusque, but shrewd. Like Sharpe, Parfitt was raised in the gutter. He worked his way up to become a wealthy industrialist, and now owns several mills.

Over dinner, Parfitt tells Sharpe that with the war over, and growing competition from foreign mills, the price of cotton is falling. The workers are restless, and some local mills have been burnt down and smashed up. Parfitt blames Matt Truman for the unrest.

Although he doesn't tell Sharpe, Parfitt is aware that he faces a more serious problem. Another dinner guest, a testy old mill-owner named Sir Percy Stanwyck, is shortly to take delivery of a steam engine that will give Parfitt some stiff competition.

Sharpe is suspicious of Parfitt and Wickham, but Stanwyck seems like an honest man. Stanwyck has heard of Sharpe from the letters of his son, a soldier who died after the battle of Talavera.

After dinner, Sharpe and Harper go in search of their billets. They quickly find that, as members of Parfitt's private security force, they are not welcome at the hostelry. When Sharpe goes for a walk that night,

With the war apparently over, Sharpe is given a posting in his native Yorkshire in command of the Scarsdale militia

guided by half-remembered memories of his childhood in the town, he is pursued and attacked. It is only the intervention of one of his former riflemen Dan Hagman – who is in the area looking for work – that saves him from serious injury.

Sharpe recognises his attacker as Truman, who regards Sharpe's new role as a betrayal of the people he grew up with. He warns Sharpe darkly to go back to his lords and ladies in London.

But Sharpe is not the quitting kind. He has a job to do, and he's going to do it. Back at the Hall, he learns from Parfitt that Truman has a price on his head of a thousand pounds. If Sharpe catches him, the reward is his.

At that moment, Saunders, Parfitt's right-hand man, arrives with news that Truman has organised an illegal gathering in a barn. The Scarsdale yeomanry are already on their way, and Sharpe goes too. But by the time they arrive, Truman has given them the slip.

Sharpe and Harper visit Keighley Workhouse, in search of records of Sharpe's late mother. There they encounter Sally Bunting, a childhood friend of Sharpe's, who reminds him that he and Truman were once close. Sally tries to persuade Sharpe to meet Truman, but to no avail.

Sharpe returns to his lodgings to be told that his 'wife' has arrived. Mystified, he enters his rooms to find Lady Anne awaiting him. Knowing that Jane has left Sharpe, Lady Anne has come hoping to resume her own affair with him. She is gently refused: Sharpe tells her he is in love with someone else.

Resigned to her loss, Lady Anne gives Sharpe some valuable information. It seems his present commission was arranged by Rossendale as a means to get Sharpe out of London. By a quirk of fate, Rossendale is currently visiting some land he has recently inherited nearby.

Not far away, Rossendale and Jane are assessing the inherited property. At first, Jane has high hopes of it generating enough money to pay

In a mock duel in Parfitt's ballroom, Sharpe's battlefield fighting skills are no match for Wickham's elegant swordplay

back what they owe Sharpe, but she quickly realises her mistake. The house is a wreck.

Parfitt holds a ball to celebrate the end of the war. Sharpe attends, and gets drawn into a show duel with Wickham, an expert swordsman, who beats him convincingly. However, Stanwyck sneers at Wickham's showiness, and publicly shames him by demanding to know where he was when Sharpe was fighting the French at Talavera.

That night, Sally takes Sharpe to the place where his mother is buried. Reading the date on her headstone, Sharpe sees that she died the day the Forlorn Hope went through the breach at the siege of Badajoz. It is an emotional moment.

Rossendale visits Shireburn Hall and tells Parfitt that Sharpe beat his wife and that he, Rossendale, had taken her in out of pity. Now, he says, Sharpe is blackmailing them to the tune of ten thousand pounds. Clearly, Rossendale is telling Parfitt, Sharpe is 'not one of us'.

A few hours later, Parfitt tells his workforce that, in the post-war slump, he's cutting wages. He warns them against sedition and promises that Major Sharpe will break up any illegal meetings and arrest the rebels' ringleader, Matt Truman. The workers look at Sharpe with ill-concealed hatred.

Parfitt himself mistrusts Sharpe. Remembering Rossendale's account of Sharpe's recent past, Parfitt reminds Sharpe who is paying him, and warns him not to be soft on the enemy.

Having discovered the whereabouts of Jane and Rossendale's new home, Sharpe pays an uninvited visit to demand the return of his money. Terrified, Jane confesses that it is nearly all spent. Sharpe leaves a message for Rossendale: 'My wife he can keep. My money I want back.' He leaves Jane sobbing.

On his return, Sharpe is met by Harper, who has news of an illegal gathering. Using rifleman's tactics rather than Wickham's cavalry ones, they arrive before Truman's look-outs raise the alarm. Sharpe issues instructions for Wickham's men to arrest Truman without loss of life.

But Wickham disobeys Sharpe's orders and his men rampage

Matt Truman warns his fellow mill workers that peace with France means confrontation with the mill owners

through the crowd, slashing and stabbing at innocent men, women and children, until the streets are running with blood. Truman and Sharpe both appeal for calm, but the crowd turns into an angry mob. One of the yeomen kicks a woman holding a child, and Hagman, now on Truman's side, pulls her assailant from the saddle and kills him. The meeting ends with Keighley Square strewn with the bodies of dead and injured workers, and Truman escaping, yelling at Sharpe as he goes that the blame for the massacre lies with him.

Appalled at the bloodshed, Sharpe and Harper go into a tavern, and find the locals so incensed that a fight seems inevitable. Even Hagman turns his back on them. Fortunately Truman arrives and calms the crowd. It is only with his help that they are able to leave unharmed.

Parfitt and Rossendale send reports to Horse Guards and plant stories in the press, making out that the massacre was Sharpe's fault. From her vantage point as the guest of Wickham, Lady Anne secretly listens to all their conversations.

Sharpe turns to Sally Bunting. From her, he learns that his mother was an alcoholic, and it was Sally and Truman who nursed her, fed her – and buried her. Finally, the penny drops. Truman is Sharpe's half-brother.

Parfitt's spies have by now discovered the same thing, and Parfitt sees an opportunity to set a trap for Truman – he will wait for Sharpe to go in search of his half-brother. When he does, Parfitt will capture them both.

Overhearing this, Lady Anne goes to warn Sharpe and tells him that she has discovered that the mills were burnt by Wickham, not Truman, as a way for Parfitt to acquire them on the cheap. Sharpe, realising that Lady Anne genuinely does care for him, capitulates to her at last and they make love.

As Parfitt predicted, Sharpe and Truman meet in secret and resolve their differences. Saunders, Parfitt's aide, discovers where they are meeting – having beaten the information out of Sally – and gives chase. In a desperate race across country, Sharpe, Harper, Hagman and

Wickham's yeomen attack a crowd of workers in Keighley Square, and despite the efforts of Sharpe and Truman to calm the situation, a peaceful meeting becomes a bloodbath

Truman are pursued by the yeomanry. As Truman bends to help Sharpe haul the exhausted Hagman across a stream, he is shot. Shouting for the others to go on without him, he dies.

Sharpe swears vengeance. He resolves to end Parfitt's corruption and to punish Wickham's insolence at one go. And, at the same time, he will repay Stanwyck for his trust and friendship, and honour the memory of his son's death at Talavera. Hagman arrives with news of Sally's beating. This adds another name to the hit-list: Saunders.

Lady Anne is sent to warn Stanwyck that his steam engine, coming by wagon from Bolton that night, will be attacked by Parfitt's thugs, posing as Truman's men. Sharpe, Harper and Hagman wait on the moors. As expected, when the wagon carrying the steam engine arrives, a dozen masked men attack and try to destroy it. Sharpe and his men attack the attackers, among them Saunders. Suddenly a masked swordsman advances on Sharpe. It is Wickham.

They fight, and as before, Wickham's elegant swordplay at first gives him the upper hand. But Sharpe drives him backwards, off the level path and onto the rough ground of the moors. Wickham struggles to keep his footing, then he falls. Sharpe stands over him, sword poised, and hisses malevolently, 'First lesson of battle. Keep your feet.'

Wickham lunges at him, and the point of his sword catches Sharpe's arm. Instead of pulling away, Sharpe advances further, taking more of the point into him. 'Second lesson of battle,' he says grimly. 'Live with the pain.'

The cavalry arrive and Wickham feigns relief, claiming that he was defending Stanwyck's steam engine from Sharpe's attack. Stanwyck is not fooled and he has Wickham arrested.

Stanwyck and Sharpe barge into Parfitt's ballroom. While Rossendale cringes fearfully in the corner, Stanwyck tells Parfitt that his days of theft and arson are over. Next, Sharpe demands that Parfitt write a letter to Horse Guards giving a true account of the massacre in Keighley Square. Then he makes Rossendale promise to obtain his release from service with the Scarsdale yeomanry.

Sharpe buries Truman, and promises Sally he won't forget them.

Jane comes to ask Sharpe to swear that he will leave her and Rossendale alone. If he refuses, Rossendale will rescind his promise to get Sharpe released from his commission. Without it, she says, he will be a deserter, fair game to be hunted down and arrested. She refuses to return Sharpe's money, telling him that England no longer needs him now the war is over. Her parting shot is that Rossendale is more of a man than Sharpe ever was. Sharpe was born in the gutter, she sneers, and that is where he belongs.

Sharpe is shaken by her onslaught. But all emotional ties between them have now been severed. He is free to return to France – and Lucille.

After a bitter confrontation, Jane leaves Sharpe for Lord Rossendale

Sir Willoughby Parfitt, Sharpe's employer, is uncovered as a liar, an arsonist and a thief

'SHARPE'S JUSTICE' CAST

SHARPE	Sean Bean
HARPER	Daragh O'Malley
JANE	Abigail Cruttenden
LADY ANNE CAMOYNES	Caroline Langrishe
TRUMAN	Philip Glenister
HAGMAN	John Tams
WICKHAM	Douglas Henshall
ROSSENDALE	Alexis Denisof
PARFITT	Tony Haygarth
SALLY BUNTING	Karen Meagher
STANWYCK	Philip Anthony
SAUNDERS	Philip Martin Brown
FOSDYKE	Sean O'Kane
WHITBREAD	Henry Moxon
MRS TRENT	Rita May
ARNOLD	Richard Bremmer
HORSE GUARDS CLERK	Tony Aitken
SAM WEST	Nick Conway
SCREENPLAY BY	Patrick Harbinson

Sharpe's Waterloo

MARCH 1815. NAPOLEON

HAS ESCAPED FROM EXILE AND RETURNED TO FRANCE

TO FIGHT FOR THE THRONE. FACING HIM ARE THE ALLIED

FORCES OF THE BRITISH, DUTCH, BELGIAN AND GERMANS

UNDER WELLINGTON, AND A PRUSSIAN ARMY

UNDER BLUECHER.

Sharpe and Lucille are working their farm when news comes that Napoleon has escaped from Elba and aims to reclaim his throne. Sharpe returns to Brussels to join Wellington for the final confrontation, and Lucille goes with him.

In Brussels, Wellington's staff are thrashing their Dutch allies at cricket, and for once Rossendale has found something he is good at. His beloved Jane may be snubbed by society, but at least he can beat the Prince of Orange at cricket.

While the officers frolic, Sharpe – recently made Lt. Col. of the 5th (Belgian) Light Dragoons – is out on reconnaissance. He unexpectedly discovers a large mass of French soldiers. He sends a dispatch to alert Wellington, but his messenger is killed.

The news that her husband is nearby appals Jane. Determined that he will not blight their lives forever, she tells Rossendale he must kill him. Although patently not up to the task, he resolves to do so.

Sharpe serves under Prince William of Orange, whose military incompetence and lack of charm makes him barely tolerated by Wellington and his deputy, Uxbridge. However, Orange's chief of staff, Rebecque, is an intelligent man, and he and Sharpe study maps and plot the positions of Napoleon's forces, trying to divine his purpose. Is Boney bluffing, prior to an attack at Mons, as Wellington has predicted? Or are the forces Sharpe has seen the main thrust of his attack? If so, it is bad news for Wellington. Sharpe believes that the crossroads at Quatre Bras is where Boney will try to split the Allied forces from their Prussian confederates. Unless the Allies can join forces with the Prussians, Napoleon will triumph. But will the Prussians arrive in time?

In conference with Rebecque at Orange's HQ, Sharpe looks up to see first Harris and Hagman, and then Harper, enter. He is delighted. He asks Doggett, one of Orange's staff officers, to put them on the strength.

French forces are still assembling and Sharpe realises he must speak to Wellington in person. He seeks out his commander at a ball, and they discuss Napoleon's position, and the uncertainties of the Prussians arriving in time. Wellington reluctantly concedes that he has indeed been humbugged. Preparations for battle must begin immediately.

On the way out, Sharpe bumps into Jane and Rossendale, frolicking in a corner. Enraged, he looks set to murder Rossendale, who is so terror-stricken that he soils himself. Blinded by rage, Sharpe is only prevented from attacking Uxbridge himself by his friend Captain Harry Price. He leaves, telling Rossendale he may keep his wife, but he must return the money he stole.

Sharpe bids Lucille farewell, and goes with Harper to the front.

Sharpe's commander at Waterloo is HRH the Prince of Orange, whose military incompetence puts his men's lives at risk

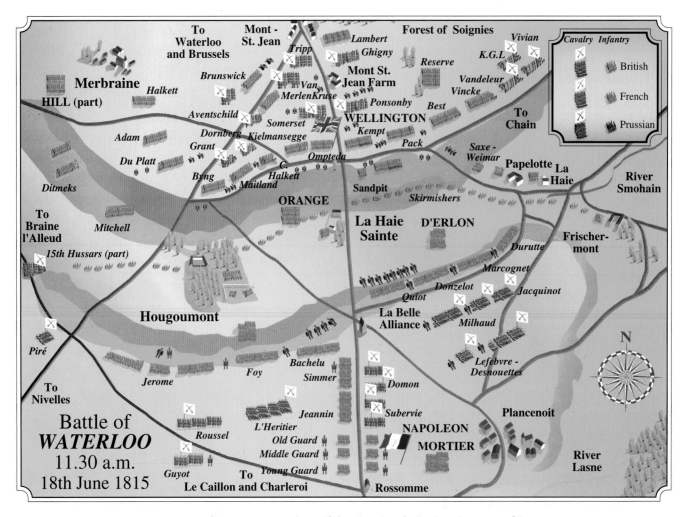

To
Waterloo
and Brussels

Mont -
St. Jean

Forest of Soignies

Lambert
Ghigny

Vivian

K.G.L

Tripp

Reserve

Merbraine

Brunswick

Mont St.
Jean Farm

Vandeleur
Vincke

HILL (part) *Halkett*

Van
MerlenKruse

Ponsonby

WELLINGTON

Best

To
Chain

Aventschild

Somerset

Kempt

Adam

Dornberg *Kielmansegge*

Pack

Saxe -
Weimar

Papelotte **La**
- Haie

Grant

Ompteda

Du Platt

C
Halkett

ORANGE

Byng

Maitland

Sandpit

River
Smohain

Ditmeks

Skirmishers

To
Braine
l'Alleud

Mitchell

La Haie
Sainte

D'ERLON

Frischer-
mont

15th Hussars (part)

Durutte

Marcognet

Donzelot

Jacquinot

Quiot

Hougoumont

Milhaud

La Belle
Alliance

Piré

Lefebvre -
Desnouettes

To
Nivelles

Bachelu
Simmer

Domon

Foy

Battle of
WATERLOO
11.30 a.m.
18th June 1815

Jerome

Jeannin

Subervie

Plancenoit

L'Heritier

Roussel

NAPOLEON

Guyot

Old Guard
Middle Guard
Young Guard

To
Le Caillon and Charleroi

MORTIER

River
Lasne

Rossomme

N

Cavalry Infantry

British

French

Prussian

The Allied forces under Wellington face those of Napoleon for the final confrontation. At its epicentre is the farm at La Haie Sainte

He arrives just as Wellington asks Orange to lend his cavalry for a major assault. With his usual bravado, Orange tries to leads the charge himself. His men refuse to follow – unlike him, they have seen a mass of French lancers hidden in the woods.

Sharpe and Harper watch as the South Essex march up. They exchange greetings with some of the men, and nod to Lt. Col. Ford who now commands them. There is still no sign of the Prussians.

The Fifth forms a square against the coming French cavalry. Orange refuses to listen to Sharpe's warning that there are French troops in dead ground, about to attack, and insists that he tell the commander of the Fifth to form his men into a line. When Sharpe refuses, he is dismissed from the field.

Sharpe rejoins the South Essex, and finds them also forming into a line, at the behest of their commander, Lt. Col. Ford. He suggests a square would be more appropriate, but Ford refuses his advice. To his horror, the French cavalry choose that moment to launch their attack,

just when the South Essex is at its most vulnerable.

Orange and Ford order their men to form squares, but it is too late. Sharpe countermands their orders, urging the men to run for their lives. It is bedlam. The colour party falls, and a French hussar makes off with the King's colours. But most of the South Essex escape, leaving Ford fulminating uselessly before he, too, finally takes to his heels.

Napoleon keeps them waiting for the main assault. Harper passes the time cooking steaks cut from dead horses, and prattling on about whether Boney is actually in the field, and where the missing Prussians might be. Beneath his light-hearted tone, the worry is evident – will the Prussians arrive in time?

Some way off, a flurry of rockets overhead frightens Rossendale's horse, and it bolts down the road towards Sharpe. Rossendale panics, and pulls out his pistol. Sharpe ignores it and walks his horse forward. When he reaches Rossendale, Sharpe disarms him and tells Rossendale that he isn't worth fighting, but he wants his money. As for Jane, says

Sharpe, where he comes from, if a woman commits adultery, her husband takes her to market and sells her off. Sneering, he offers Rossendale a rope with which to take Jane to market.

The waiting continues. During the lull, Sharpe makes a formal apology to the Prince of Orange – he can't afford not to – and listens while Orange pontificates about where he will be stationed tomorrow. It will be at the farm of La Haie Sainte.

Back at his base, Rossendale tries to pass off his broken weapons as the result of a fray with some French lancers. But he can't keep up the pretence, and confesses to his friend Witherspoon his unenviable dilemma – either he loses Jane, or he kills Sharpe. And he knows he cannot kill Sharpe. Before Witherspoon can offer his own sword so that at least his friend can die like a man, Rossendale has fled.

It is dawn, and Sharpe visits his men to encourage them. Unfortunately, so does Orange, and Sharpe is forced to endure one more of his commander's pointless homilies. Then Sharpe and Rebecque bid each other good luck, and set off to take up their stations.

Sharpe and Harper recce La Haie Sainte and are amazed to find it entirely unprepared for defence. Soldiers are trying to scratch loopholes in the thick walls of the farmhouse with their bayonets, their trenching tools having been lost the previous day. And the farmhouse gates, which would have been their first line of defence against the

hordes of oncoming French, have been burnt for fuel. These are being replaced by a makeshift barricade of carts and ploughs.

There is mounting tension about the day ahead, and Sharpe predicts that until the Prussians arrive, the Allied forces are heavily outnumbered by those of Napoleon and will inevitably suffer huge losses. There are moments of sadness – as Rebecque and Sharpe wish one another joy of the day, knowing that neither one may survive it – and humour, as Orange once again shows his incompetence and Sharpe jokes with Hagman that someone ought to shoot the future king of the Netherlands.

Up on the ridge, Wellington orders his officers to make ready as the French start up their military bands. Finally, Wellington's staff sight Napoleon and the first cannon shot is heard from the French. The battle has begun. Wellington orders the men to take cover by lying down. All around the field, soldiers in their thousands obey.

Back at the farm, the screaming starts almost immediately. The French advance. Sharpe, Hagman and Harris skirmish and shoot some of the first arrivals. The Allies begin to fire and the French line pauses for a moment. Sharpe pulls his men back into the farm.

They take up firing positions, and the French press the gate hard. The first man through is a huge bearded sapeur of the 54th. As the French pour into the courtyard, it is every man for himself. Harris and Hagman scale the roof and fire down into the courtyard. Sharpe follows

Two stranded French cavalrymen run the gauntlet of properly-formed Allied infantry squares on the field at Waterloo

three French soldiers into the stables where the wounded have been brought, kills two and narrowly avoids death at the hands of a third.

Someone has closed the gates, and the English round on the French, now trapped inside the courtyard, picking them off one by one. Slowly, the sound of gunfire dies away.

But not for long. Sharpe climbs the barricade, and sees Orange once more forming his men into lines, leaving them at the mercy of the French cavalry. Predictably, they are slaughtered in their scores.

The men inside La Haie Sainte throw open the gates to let in Orange and Rebecque, and the gates are closed behind them, leaving the men outside to their fate.

Sharpe's rage is terrible to behold. He curses Orange, and calls for the gates to be opened so he can leave. When Orange orders his men to arrest Sharpe, the men ignore him. Sharpe and Harper are able to leave.

They ride along the road strewn with the bodies of Red Germans and 54th French, Harris and Hagman jogging behind. But it is not in the nature of any of them to walk away from a battle. The French are about to attack again, and Harris and Hagman pause for a moment, then turn and go back. Sharpe and Harper follow.

From his vantage point above the field, Wellington orders the men to rise. All around the field, men get to their feet and form lines. Orders are given: 'Present! Fire!' and there is the almighty crash of musket fire. Wellington orders out the Heavies, and Uxbridge and Rossendale ride forward with them. Rossendale finally finds the courage to fight, but within minutes, he is speared by a French lancer. He dies, screaming.

In Brussels, in their separate homes, Jane and Lucille listen to the distant sound of battle. Lucille waits anxiously for news. Jane, who has discovered herself to be pregnant, has morning sickness. She does not yet know that the child's father has been killed in battle, and she faces destitution.

Ford and Harry Price are yelling and rallying the men. Orange panics, and tries to escape from the courtyard, followed by Rebecque and Doggett. Clearing the way for him are Hagman and Harris, fighting with fixed bayonets, doing as much damage as they can. But Orange is concerned only for his own safety. He deserts them, and Hagman falls to the ground. Harris drops to defend him from a French soldier, and is bayonetted from behind. Hagman is shot in the head. They die, reaching for

The death of two heroes: Hagman falls, and as Harris goes to his rescue, he is bayonetted from behind by a French soldier

In the closing moments of the battle Sharpe glimpses Napoleon for the first — and last — time

each other, while Orange, Rebecque and Doggett ride free.

From the ridge, Wellington sees his opponent throw his own Imperial Guard into the fray. Truly, Napoleon has given up the battle.

When Sharpe learns of the deaths of Hagman and Harris, he goes back to avenge their loss. Despite Harper's best attempts to prevent it, Sharpe picks up his rifle, lines up Orange in his sights, and squeezes off a round. Orange sags forward on the neck of his horse.

Now Harper sees the Imperial Guard in the field, and knows this is the end. He and Sharpe run back up the ridge to the South Essex. Sharpe forms them up and has them fire again and again into the ranks of the Imperial Guard. The South Essex advance, with Sharpe at their head, and out of the smoke and din Wellington rides up, urging them on and telling him the Imperial Guard will not stand. The South Essex go forward. And finally, as the Prussians arrive at last and the Guards fall back, Sharpe sees the unmistakable figure of Napoleon through the smoke of battle. As he watches, Boney turns and leaves the field, defeated at last.

Days later, Sharpe returns to Normandy. Alone, he trudges down the path to a small farmhouse. In the distance waits the tiny figure of Lucille. As he nears her, he takes off his tricorne, waves it, and then tosses it high up into the sky and away. Then he breaks into the long, loping jog of the rifleman, and runs towards Lucille. And home.

'SHARPE'S WATERLOO' CAST

SHARPE	Sean Bean
HARPER	Daragh O'Malley
JANE	Abigail Cruttenden
ROSSENDALE	Alexis Denisof
LUCILLE	Cecile Paoli
WELLINGTON	Hugh Fraser
PRINCE WILLIAM OF ORANGE	Paul Bettany
REBECQUE	Oliver Tobias
UXBRIDGE	Neil Dickson
HARRY PRICE	Nicholas Irons
MACDUFF	Martin Cochrane
HARRIS	Jason Salkey
HAGMAN	John Tams
DOGGETT	Martin Glyn Murray
WITHERSPOON	Owen Brenman
LT. COL. FORD	Shaughan Seymour
DUCHESS OF RICHMOND	Jane Merrow
PAULETTE	Chloe Newsome
DUTCH CAPTAIN	Janek Lesniak
SCREENPLAY BY	Charles Wood

Sharpe's World

Despite what the recruiters might say, life in Wellington's army was no holiday. Accounts of the time show that discipline was harsh, food short and battles bloody.

LIFE IN THE ARMY

t the dawn of the nineteenth century, the British army was in a period of transition. After the humiliations of the American War of Independence, its more far-sighted commanders were beginning to re-think the strategy of using soldiers as little more than a well-disciplined battering ram. They argued that the soldier should be trained to think for himself, and that discipline should be achieved by pride and consent, rather than naked terror.

Among the fruits of this new thinking were the 95th Rifles. Formed in 1800 as an experimental corps and trained by – among others – Major-General Sir John Moore, the 95th were schooled to outwit and out-manoeuvre the enemy by a combination of teamwork and use of their own initiative.

Instead of fighting in large formation like the Redcoats, the Rifles were deployed in small groups, skirmishing, sniping and scouting, using any cover they could find. It was their proud boast that they were

always first into the field and last out of it. Indeed it was a subaltern in the 95th who had the unfortunate honour of being the first British soldier to be killed in the Peninsular War, on the 15th August, 1808.

The flexible organisation of the 95th enabled them to exploit the range and accuracy of the Baker rifle to the full. Paradoxically, Napoleon's mistrust of the rifle – it was as liable as the musket to misfire, and slower to load – led him to withdraw all rifles from the French forces in 1804, putting his soldiers in Spain at a permanent disadvantage, not just from skirmishers, but also from Spanish guerrilleros.

Meanwhile, the 95th went from strength to strength, and by the end of the War had earned its reputation as one of the elite regiments of the British army. Its name changed to the Rifle Brigade in 1815. Today, its descendants are better known as the Royal Green Jackets.

Clad in dark green uniforms that camouflaged them in the field, the Rifles looked so smart and dashing that the mere sight of them was enough to persuade the diminutive son of a West Country shepherd named Harris, then a young conscript in the light company of the 66th, to volunteer for the second battalion.

And it is fortunate for us that he did, for Harris' chronicle of his duties with the Rifles – not just as a fighting man, but also as the regiment's chief cobbler – is one of the most vivid autobiographical accounts of the time.

Another useful eyewitness account of the War is that of a man named Thomas. Thomas joined the 71st Highland regiment of foot in a fit of pique when his acting career went awry. He soon realised his mistake, and his graphic tales of military life are punctuated by heartfelt regrets for his moment of rashness.

In battle, a light infantryman might have to fire over a hundred rounds of ball-cartridge in a day, while stepping over the bodies of his dead and injured comrades. At the end of the day, his shoulder would be blackened and bruised from the recoil of his musket. Fighting in close order, the infantry were also vulnerable to opposing fire. Harris once saw a single cannon-ball kill three men at once, and there were instances of up to ten men standing in file meeting their end this way.

However, fighting en masse did mean that the infantry were better able to protect themselves from enemy horse. Hence the practice of

John Mollo's costume designs for riflemen of the 95th. The dark green uniforms camouflaged them in the field

Fighting in close order, redcoats often had to fire over a hundred rounds in a single day

Formed in squares with bayonets fixed, the massed ranks of the infantry withstood many a cavalry charge

forming a square, with bayonets fixed, when under attack by cavalry. At Waterloo, the 71st successfully beat off seven cavalry attacks in this manner.

Field-guns firing canister or round shot were used by both sides, though much of the French artillery was of a heavier calibre than that of the Allies. The British had the benefit of Major Shrapnel's invention of a shell that burst over the heads of the enemy in a shower of musket balls, and – when it worked – of Sir William Congreve's explosive rocket. All of these used black powder, which gave off a dense grey smoke that effectively prevented the soldier from knowing his position, or what danger lay ahead.

Between battles, the men would have to march – often as far as 40 miles in a day – carrying all their possessions on their backs. Each man would carry greatcoat, blanket, camp kettle, ship-biscuit and beef, a

canteen full of water, hatchet, rifle and 80 rounds of ball cartridge on his back. When it rained, the blanket and greatcoat became sodden and even heavier.

As chief shoemaker to the regiment, Harris also had to heft the tools of his trade – minus the lapstone, that is, which he 'took the liberty of flinging to the devil'.

Even ordinarily encumbered, the sheer weight of their packs exhausted the men, and impeded movement on the march and in combat. In the extreme heat of summer campaigns, many soldiers fainted and even died under the weight of their packs. And if a man fell to the ground, he often needed the assistance of another soldier to get back on his feet.

But it was in winter that conditions were at their worst. With bad weather, poor shelter, and little food, who'd be a soldier?

WINTER CAMPAIGNS

he retreat to Coruña during the winter of 1808 was one of the most arduous journeys ever undertaken by a British army. So cold that the men woke in the morning to find their hair and beards white with frost, the march took its toll of both men and officers. Reeling with fatigue, riddled with vermin, many bootless, the men were barely able to keep going themselves, let alone aid those of their comrades and families who collapsed and froze to death by the wayside, to be picked off by the pursuing French or eaten by wolves.

Miserable, angry and humiliated, says Thomas, the soldiers would rather have turned and stood at bay to fight the enemy than endure this mortifying withdrawal.

Many times on that terrible march, Harris saw men and women collapse by the side of the road, and await their death – be it from cold, hunger or the ravages of the enemy. He himself crashed to the ground on more than one occasion, and it was only a combination of his own iron constitution, the occasional lucky find of food or shelter, and the support of a friend, that got him back on his feet and kept him going.

When they finally reached the beach where the army was to be picked up by the navy, Harris was so exhausted that he almost missed the disembarkation. Unable to stand without the support of his rifle, but too weak to call out for help, he was only saved because a lieutenant already at sea spotted him alone on the shore and made the boat return to collect him.

And even then, his troubles were not over. A tremendous gale blew up that night, and the ship he was in turned over. It was not until six hours later that the sea grew calm, and the ship magically righted herself.

Harris had seen six hundred of his fellow riflemen left dead or dying on the way, and he himself had been nearly blinded by the conditions.

On the long retreat to Coruña in the winter of 1808, the pursuing French preferred to pick off stragglers rather than face the massed guns of the British redcoats

LIFE ON THE ROAD

Throughout that long march, the wives and lovers of the men had had to keep up as best they could, and although they were women they were not accorded many privileges with regard to food or shelter.

Many died. But mysteriously, some of those who seemed most vulnerable survived. Harris saw a woman who was heavily pregnant fall out of line with her husband and lie down in the snow. Thinking she had given up the struggle, he was surprised to see her a few hours later, hurrying with her husband towards the embarkation point. In her arms was a newborn baby.

Despite the evident strength of some of the camp followers, as a result of the burden caused by the women on the Retreat, the allowance of wives was greatly restricted on future campaigns, and many wives were left behind. When the men set off, many had to be forcibly parted from their wives.

Equally sad partings were endured when the army was disbanded in 1814 in France after the war. The men returned to their home countries, but their Spanish and Portuguese wives and lovers – women who had supported them so loyally, and who had endured so much on their behalf – were rigidly sent home to Spain and Portugal.

Harris gives a touching account of events after the battle of Roliça, when he helped a distraught woman search for the body of her dead husband, a former comrade of his named Cochran. When they found Cochran's corpse, the widow's grief so moved Harris that he had another man help him bury the body.

Even though widowed, Mrs Cochran continued to follow her late husband's company as far as Lisbon, where she intended to get a passage home. In the weeks that followed, Harris did his best to see that she received food and comfort, and the two became friends. However, she declined his offer of marriage. Having been so distressed by the sight of her dead husband, she said, she was set against marrying another soldier.

The terrible conditions of the long winter marches led men who were formerly friends to revert to more basic concerns. Thomas graphically describes how he and his comrades plumbed the depths of human despair on the long march from Villafranca to Castro. Drenched, famished, frozen and exhausted beyond endurance, each man regarded his neighbour with a look that seemed to say, 'One or other of the articles you wear would be of great use to me; your shoes are better than those I possess; if you were dead, they would be mine.'

Every night, each man slept with his belongings clutched to his chest, or tied to his arm, desperately trying to protect his meagre possessions from theft by men he called his friends.

Sure enough, on arrival at Lugo, when Thomas finally got some sleep, he awoke to find his little store of bread gone. His response was to look around for a fellow soldier the worse for drink, and pilfer the beef and bread from his haversack.

Warmth was also a problem. Thomas and the 71st were reduced to burning shoes found in enemy stores at Astorga during the winter of 1808. 'Though a fourth of the army were in want of them, and I among the rest, yet they were consumed alongst with the other stores in the magazines.'

The winter of 1813, pursuing the forces of Marshal Soult across the Pyrenees and into France, was another severe test. The winds were so strong that, for several days and nights, the men could not get a tent to stand. Frostbite was commonplace, and the cold was so severe that men died at their posts without a sound. The 92nd Highlanders were issued with grey flannel trousers – even the hardy Scots would have frozen to death in their kilts.

Harper's wife, Ramona, was a camp follower

On these long winter marches, a weakness for drink could be fatal. Many a soldier, having drunk his daily half pint of grog, lay down in the snow to sleep it off and never woke. Many more, staggering drunkenly behind, were cut down by the French, who persistently harried the lines, but rarely dared to confront them. Well aware of their men's propensity for drink, the British commanders sometimes deliberately holed barrels of liquor, or even camped in the cold and rain outside a town, rather than risk the men storming the wine stores and drinking themselves insensible.

Unusually for a Redcoat, the fastidious Thomas was not fond of drinking – particularly after an incident at Mafra which put him off wine for life. The British were following the retreating French as they left Sobral, and Thomas and his friends had found a large tun of wine in a wine-store. They climbed the ladder propped against its side, and buckled their canteen straps together to lower a camp kettle down inside and so draw up some wine. They all drank, but when the kettle went down a second time, it got caught on something in the bottom of the tun. Lowering a lighted candle to inspect the obstruction, they found the body of a dead French soldier lying in the wine. What little liking Thomas had for red wine disappeared altogether after that.

JOINING UP

John Mollo's designs for the uniform of a sergeant in the 95th Rifles

ack in England, not long after the terrible retreat from Coruña had so depleted their forces, the 95th needed to replenish their numbers.

Unlike the Navy, the Army had no press-gang system, but relied upon generous bounties to entice men to join up – sometimes as much as eleven guineas for signing up for seven years. To a simple village labourer, this must have seemed like a fortune. But it would have seemed less plentiful by the time deductions had been made for 'necessaries', and the 'volunteers' had paid for the drink that invariably accompanied recruiting sprees.

The Rifles picked Harris and a sergeant-major for their recruiting drive. Dressed in their finest, the two Riflemen toured the tap-rooms of Rye and Lydd to try to coax some of the militias to join them.

When they chanced upon the Leicester Militia, who were quartered in Hastings, they discovered someone else had got there first. No less than 125 men and two officers had already volunteered for the 7th Fusiliers.

Undeterred, the two Riflemen set about changing the men's minds.

Giving each volunteer two guineas bounty, Harris and his sergeant-major kept up a riot of partying and drinking for three days and nights. Then they marched every one of the 127 men off to join the 95th.

Recruitment was easier for the dashing Rifles than for some of the less glamorous regiments, whose colonels sometimes had to use their own funds to encourage recruits. There are accounts of crimpers (professional recruiters) hiring prostitutes and equipping them with handcuffs with which to pin their newfound 'volunteers' to the bed in case they changed their minds overnight.

Some units derived their character from the type of men they recruited. The Brunswick Oels Jägers, for example, were formed in England in 1809 from a number of European refugees who had fought Jerome Bonaparte under the Duke of Brunswick. Included in their ranks were Poles, Danes, Swiss, Dutch and Croats as well as Germans, most of whom had been languishing in British prison camps, and had obtained their release in exchange for service against Napoleon.

CRIME AND PUNISHMENT

Harris often records the punishments meted out for various infringements of the rules. One of his own earliest memories is of being in the firing party that executed a man who had volunteered and absconded with his bounty no less than 16 times.

A more usual punishment was a flogging. Despite increasing popular concern regarding the inhumanity of the lash, we hear of two men receiving 700 lashes, one for misappropriating army funds, and the other for desertion. Interestingly, although he regarded the lash as brutish, Harris remained convinced that the British army could not survive without it.

The French were not as well disciplined as the British, and Thomas contends that the French officers would have to spur their men on by example, exhorting them into the very teeth of the enemy. In contrast, he says, their British counterparts would more often be restraining their men, bidding them hold their fire until the French were nearly upon them. As Thomas remarks, "'Steady, lads, steady' is all you hear, and that in an undertone."

He even tells of the French General Girard who, finding his forces overtaken by the British in a town named Arroyo dos Molinos, vented his rage by throwing his cocked hat on the ground and jumping up and down on it so violently that all the medals fell off his coat. Girard's reaction might be forgiven in view of the enormous losses incurred on that occasion – despite their powder being too wet to fire, the Redcoats took 3,000 prisoners that day.

The behaviour of the French off the battlefield earned them the undying enmity of both Portuguese and Spanish people. When the 71st pursued the retreating French from Sobral to Santerem, Thomas saw such a trail of arson, atrocities and murder that he wondered why God did not sweep the Frenchman from the face of the earth.

The Portuguese took bloody revenge on any French soldier they could catch. After a battle, any man who still had some life in him was liable to be chased, tortured and killed. Even the corpses were mutilated.

Despite this, there are many documented occasions of kindnesses rendered across the battle lines.

It was customary after a battle for both sides to collect their respective wounded under a flag of truce, so men who, a few hours earlier, had been blazing away at each other would be side by side, searching for their fallen comrades. On one such occasion, Harris records giving water to a dying Frenchman, although he was roundly derided by a fellow Rifleman for doing so.

Thomas tells of the 50th, the 71st and the 92nd being quartered for five weeks in Sabreira, with little to do but mount picquets, dig defences and drill. The enemy were only 150 yards away, doing much the same thing. However, the French were very short of provisions. On the day in question, they were just about to slaughter a bullock that they had procured earlier when it broke free and blundered into British lines. The Redcoats gleefully butchered the beast and settled down to roast it – in full view of the ravenous French. After a while, a French officer came across under a flag of truce and petitioned humbly for a half share of the meat. He was given it.

Thomas had personal experience of French kindness when he was wounded at Toulouse. Falling in the heat of battle, he saw a French soldier advancing on him, and prepared himself for death. Suddenly, another Frenchmen ordered his comrades not to fire. This man remembered having been saved from a Portuguese soldier by Thomas at Sobral some months before, and he was returning the favour. Touchingly, before he departed, Thomas' new friend gave him a pancake that he had stored in his hat – though this didn't prevent one of the French rearguard from relieving Thomas of his knapsack as he passed.

Looting from the dead and wounded – of both sides – was usual after a battle, and, with a little practice, Harris became adept at rifling the lining of the uniforms of dead Frenchmen in search of money and other valuables.

Food and water were usually in desperately short supply, and Harris once had reason to be grateful to three dead Frenchmen after one particular battle for providing him with both commodities. Although their bodies had already been stripped of valuables, the looters had overlooked their victims' biscuits. Harris was not so careless – he collected the biscuits, scraped off the blood with his bayonet, and ate them hungrily.

Some men were not above stealing from the dead of their own side, too. Harris relates that a fellow rifleman, finding himself unable to remove a ring from the dead hand of one of his own officers, hacked off the finger. The perpetrator was subsequently given 500 lashes.

British soldiers caught stealing from civilians were also severely punished. Well aware of the need for co-operation from the local populace, Wellington ordered that all food was to be purchased. Although tremendously difficult to organise, it was a sound policy that endeared

The French army helped itself to food, shelter and horses wherever it went. In contrast, Wellington's practice of paying for supplies, while expensive, reaped dividends in terms of popular support

his army to the Spanish and the Portuguese.

The French populace, accustomed to their own army helping itself – legally – to food, horses and shelter, also appreciated this policy. And even though the coffers were empty and Wellington's army was forced to pay for French food in counterfeit coin, it was coin that was indistinguishable from the original.

Disobedience was rife, of course, and usually severely punished. However, Thomas recounts one occasion in which theft was not punished. His colonel was berating a number of men for stealing flour from a mill while their fellows were working. As he did so, a hen that the colonel himself had stolen and tucked into his jacket put her head out of his coat pocket and looked about. This reduced the men to gales of laughter. Fortunately for them, the colonel saw the funny side, and abandoned the punishment.

Harris endorsed the strict discipline of officers such as General Craufurd who enforced punishment for theft and insubordination, even though the French were on his heels. Discipline was vital, says Harris, if Craufurd flogged two, he saved hundreds by his management.

OFFICERS AND GENTLEMEN

Although individuals got promoted for acts of bravery, promotion from the ranks was not a frequent event. Possibly as few as 5% of officers in the Peninsular army rose from humble origins.

More often, promotion was the result of a judicious combination of money and lobbying, and the warring factions in the War Office and Horse Guards made politicking vital to personal advancement.

The venality of this system reached its nadir with the notorious scandal of 1809. Mary Anne Clarke, then the mistress of the Duke of York, who was Commander in Chief, was discovered to have been selling commissions. Her system was simple – officers paid her cash, and she persuaded York to make the appointments. On occasions when he forgot, she pinned reminders to the curtains of his bed. When the scandal

Wellington's military genius was the result of administrative expertise as well as martial skill

broke, York – even though he had never profited from the arrangement himself – was forced to resign, and it was not until two years later that he was once again able to put his considerable administrative skills to the service of his country.

Despite such scandals, the British soldier seems to have preferred to be commanded by officers who were well-born rather than those promoted from the ranks. Bravery in the field was important, but so too were good manners and kindness towards the men. Harris observed that an act of compassion done by an officer one day was often the cause of his life being saved in battle the next.

The Duke of Wellington himself, incontestably Britain's greatest military commander at the time, bought his early promotions.

Born into the wealthy Wellesley family, Arthur grew up in the shadow of his elder brother, Richard, and showed no early military promise.

Wellesley obtained an infantry commission in 1787, and was aide-de-camp to the Lord Lieutenant of Ireland until 1793. He became Lieutenant Colonel of the 33rd Foot in 1793, and commanded the regiment in the Duke of York's Netherlands Campaign the following year. While there, he was shocked by the ineptitude of his fellow officers, and began to study military matters in depth.

Wellesley served in India from 1797 to 1805, developing his skills as a civil administrator as well as an eye for careful reconnaissance and logistics. An austere and somewhat humourless man, he was known for his rigid intolerance of corruption – a stance that did not always endear him to his fellow officers.

Wellesley's military achievements against Napoleon are well-documented in the *Sharpe* books and films, but victory at Waterloo by no means represented the end of his career.

Having been MP for Rye before his military career, Wellington – Wellesley was enobled after Talavera – was no stranger to political life. Once home, he re-entered politics, becoming a cabinet member in 1818. He reluctantly became Prime Minister in 1828, and later held office as Home Secretary, Foreign Secretary and once again as Premier. He remained Commander in Chief until 1852, the year of his death.

France, too, had its outstanding commanders. Two of these were Marshals Soult and Ney.

Soult was one of the most persistent of Wellington's adversaries. Born the son of a Gascon notary, he joined the Bourbon infantry in 1785 and rose rapidly through the ranks, amassing titles and wealth as he went. Regarded by Napoleon as the best tactician in Europe, he fought at Coruña, Oporto, Ocaña and – on three separate occasions – Badajoz, blockaded Cadiz and re-took Madrid. After Vitoria, Soult took command of all Napoleon's forces, and succeeded in holding off the Allies' advance into France for a full ten months, until his defeat at Toulouse. After Waterloo, he was exiled, but his rank was restored in 1820 and he went on to be Minister of War (twice), Minister of Foreign Affairs, and Marshal-General of France. He died in 1851, at the age of 82.

Like Soult, the fiery red-headed Marshal Ney came from humble beginnings. He began his military career as a hussar. He accompanied Massena in the invasion of Portugal, took Ciudad Rodrigo, cleared the Coa and fought at Bussaco. Ney battled tenaciously during the invasion of Russia, and throughout 1814, but eventually became an advocate of Napoleon's abdication. Despite defecting to the Bourbons – during whose brief reign in 1815 he was Commander in Chief of the cavalry and a peer of France – Ney later returned to Napoleon's side and was made battle commander at Waterloo. But if he had hoped for a peaceful retirement afterwards, he was disappointed. The Bourbons had him arrested and, ignoring even Wellington's appeal for clemency, had him executed on 4 December 1815.

Napoleon relied heavily on two of his commanders: Marshals Soult and Ney. They both rose through the ranks to fight by his side

MARCHING HOME

Effective as these commanders were, disease and surgery were responsible for more soldiers' deaths than battle itself. Be that as it may, however, they did their best under appalling conditions. Army surgeons became expert at performing rapid amputations. After the battle of Vimeiro, Harris saw a pile of some 20 amputated legs – many of which were still clothed – outside the hospital.

Early in the war, thousands of Allied soldiers fell victim to a form of malaria contracted in the disastrous Walcheren expedition of 1809. What became known as 'Walcheren Fever' wiped out 4,000 men.

Although he did not succumb immediately, Harris eventually caught Walcheren Fever and was an invalid for many months. He never made a full recovery, but his military experience and record – to say nothing of his cobbling skills – meant the army could ill afford to lose him. In 1814, he was appointed to the 8th Veteran Battalion, where he spent four months among the halt and the lame before Napoleon was exiled to Elba, and Harris's battalion was disbanded. Harris was eventually discharged with a pension of 6d a day – a pension that he lost after failing to answer the call-up when Napoleon escaped from Elba and attempted to re-take France.

Thomas, too, got Walcheren Fever, and as he lay sweating in his hospital bed, he was sickened to see the orderlies squabbling over the possessions of men not yet dead. Despite this he did return to his regiment to fight at Waterloo. In 1815, after the discharge he had longed for so much and so often, he returned to his native Edinburgh. As he sailed into port, he was too upset by the sight of home to remain on deck, and he went below. Alone in the city, he felt awkward and uncertain, and was further distressed by arriving at his old house to find his family had moved away and were no longer known there.

Going into a tavern, he was recognised by the landlord, who was kind enough to send for his mother, and at last they were reunited. Throughout his eight years under arms, he had so often dreamed of this moment.

Sadly, though, Thomas was unable to find work afterwards, and appears to have emigrated. During the years that followed the war, he found civilian life harsh – so much so that, in his last letter to a friend, written in 1818, Thomas even wrote that he wished he were a soldier once again.

TALAVERA

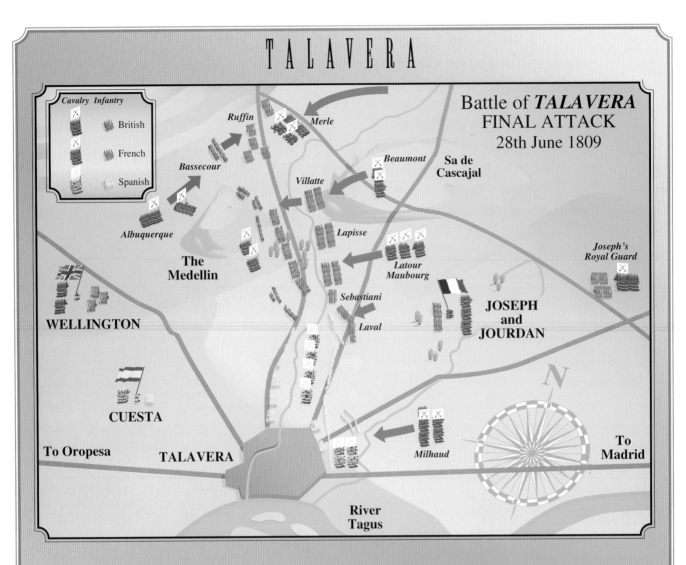

Battle of *TALAVERA*
FINAL ATTACK
28th June 1809

Cavalry Infantry
British
French
Spanish

Ruffin

Merle

Bassecour

Beaumont

Sa de
Cascajal

Villatte

Albuquerque

Lapisse

Joseph's
Royal Guard

The
Medellin

Latour
Maubourg

WELLINGTON

Sebastiani

JOSEPH
and
JOURDAN

Laval

CUESTA

N

To Oropesa

TALAVERA

Milhaud

To
Madrid

River
Tagus

• JULY 1809 •

Considered by Wellington one of his most bitter battles, Talavera saw 55,500 Allied soldiers and 60 guns – including 34,800 Spaniards led by General Cuesta – go into battle against a force of 46,150 French troops and 80 guns under Joseph Bonaparte and Marshal Jourdan.

Wellesley (as he was at the time) withdrew his entire force west of the River Alberche. By the afternoon of 27 July, the Allied forces were holding a line with entrenchments. A division of French launched a surprise attack against the key British position after dark, and it was not until 11pm that night that General Hill's counter-attack drove the French back.

At 5am, after an uneasy night, Joseph and Jourdan launched 40,000 men against the British section of the line. But three French columns and 30 guns were repulsed.

In the full heat of a July day, the French attacked three times, and though they were repelled by Sherbrooke's superior fire-power, he was unable to press his advance. Wellesley held the centre, and another French advance attempted to turn the Allied flank at the north. A brave cavalry charge by Anson's brigade met with disaster when the 23rd Light Dragoons charged into a ravine and had to be extricated by the King's German Legion.

Finally, the French retreated, and the battle was over. The British had lost 5,365 men – a quarter of their strength – and the Spaniards 1,200. The French lost 7,268. Sadly, many wounded perished in a brush fire that tore across the tinder-dry plain.

Aware that Marshal Soult was advancing to envelop him from the north, planning to cut him off from Portugal, Wellesley decided to retire to the west. He was later made a viscount for his conduct of the battle.

THE SIEGE OF BADAJOZ

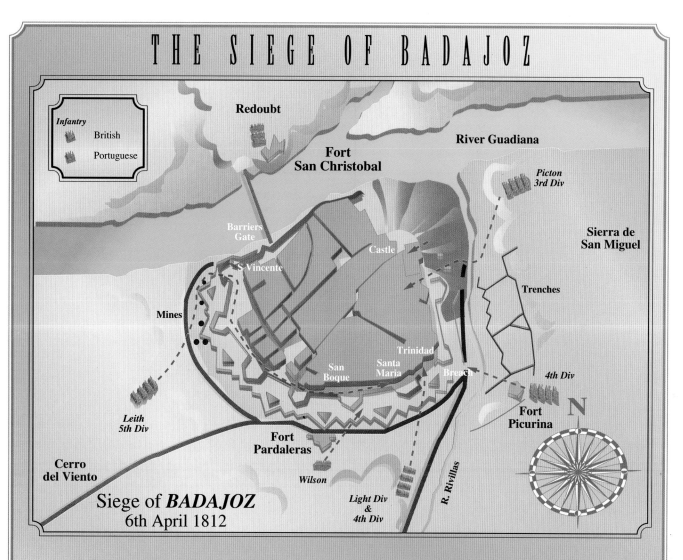

Siege of **BADAJOZ**
6th April 1812

Labels on map: Redoubt · Fort San Christobal · River Guadiana · Picton 3rd Div · Sierra de San Miguel · Barriers Gate · Castle · S Vincente · Trenches · Mines · Trinidad · Santa Maria · San Boque · Breach · 4th Div · Leith 5th Div · Fort Picurina · Fort Pardaleras · Wilson · Light Div & 4th Div · R. Rivillas · R. Rivillas · Cerro del Viento · N

Legend: Infantry — British — Portuguese

• JANUARY-APRIL 1812 •

The fortified town of Badajoz was a key location for both the French and the Allies since it guarded the Spanish side of the southern corridor between Portugal and Spain. Besieged four times during the Peninsular war, it fell to Soult in March 1811, and the following May both Beresford and Wellington were forced to abandon attempts to recapture it after only a few days.

Wellington made another attempt the following year, placing four divisions to cover the operation and four more in the siege lines. The Allies took the town on 16 March, quickly followed by an outlying post at Fort Picurina, which offered an excellent position from which their guns could concentrate fire on the weakest section of the fortress perimeter, the southeastern wall.

Wellington battered at three separate breaches, and on the night of 6 April, sent the 4th and Light Divisions to storm them.

At the same time, the 3rd was dispatched to storm the castle by escalade (scaling fortified walls with ladders), and the 5th – with Portuguese help – to mount a diversion.

Wellington's 'forlorn hope' and 40 other assaults were repulsed by General Phillipon's careful defences. Fortunately, the 3rd succeeded in taking the castle by 11.30pm, and the 5th entered by the northwest side. Both divisions forced their way through the town and attacked the rear of the French forces defending the breach. Phillipon retreated into Fort San Christobal on the far bank of the river, but surrendered the next day.

Wellington lost 3,350 men at Badajoz, and a further 1,410 in the preparatory stages – numbers that dwarfed the French casualties of 1,350 out of a defending force of 5,000. Following the assault, the Allied soldiers sacked the town, and it took Wellington three days to regain control of his men.

SHARPE'S RIFLES and SHARPE'S EAGLE

A CELTIC/ PICTURE PALACE
PRODUCTION FOR CENTRAL
FILMED: AUGUST - DECEMBER 1992
TRANSMITTED: MAY 1993

Director ... Tom Clegg
Producer ... Malcolm Craddock
Executive Producers ... Ted Childs
... Muir Sutherland
Casting ... John and Ros Hubbard
Music ... Dominic Muldowney
... John Tams
Production Designer ... Andrew Mollo
Costume Designer ... John Mollo
Director of Photography ... Ivan Strasburg
Editor ... Robin Sales
Associate Producer ... Neville Thompson
1st Assistant Director ... Marc Jenny
2nd Assistant Director ... Sam Craddock
Production Manager (Portugal) ... Chris Thompson
Unit Manager ... Christian Abomnes
Production Co-ordinator ... Winnie Wishart
Script Supervisor ... Pat Rambaut
Producer's Assistant ... Cindy Winter
Director's Assistant ... Irene Meldris
Production Accountant ... Lesley Broderick
Script Editor ... Gina Cronk
Camera Operator ... Richard Philpott
Focus ... Mark Strasburg
Grip ... Dennis Lloyd
Gaffer ... Yuri Nugis
Sound Recordist ... Christian Wangler
Sound Mixer ... Colin Martin
Boom Operator ... David Lis
Art Directors ... Philip Elton
... Vladimir Litvinov
Set Dressers ... Irina Sapozhnikova
... Alison Stewart-Richardson
Props ... Colin Thurston
Asst. Costume Designer ... Barbara Rutter
Wardrobe Supervisor ... Helen Khramova
Chief Make-up ... Margarida Miranda
Chief hairdresser ... Sano de Perpessac
Dubbing Editor ... Colin Chapman
Assistant Editor ... Adam Boome
Stunt Co-ordinator ... Greg Powell
... Sasha Philatov
Horse Master ... Slava Burlachko
Horse Stunt Co-ordinator ... Oleg Keratin
Technical Advisor ... Richard Moore
Special Effects Supervisor ... Goby Evitsky
Titles ... Baxter Hobbins Sides

FILMED IN THE CRIMEA WITH THE EAST-WEST
CREATIVE ASSOCIATION
Stepan Pojenian, Pavel Douvidson, Igor Nossov,
John Raymond, Tatyana Shakhgeldian,
Victor Voronoy, Caroline McManus

FILMED IN PORTUGAL WITH ANIMEDIA
AUDIOVISUAL
Patricia Vieira, Jose Correia

SHARPE'S COMPANY, SHARPE'S ENEMY and SHARPE'S HONOUR

A CELTIC/ PICTURE PALACE
PRODUCTION FOR CENTRAL
FILMED: AUGUST - DECEMBER 1993
TRANSMITTED: MAY - JUNE 1994

Director ... Tom Clegg
Producer ... Simon Lewis
Executive Producers ... Ted Childs
... Malcolm Craddock
... Muir Sutherland
Casting ... John and Ros Hubbard
... Lisa-Anne Porter
Music ... Dominic Muldowney,
... John Tams
Prouction Designer ... Andrew Mollo
Costume Designer ... Robin Fraser Paye
Director of Photography ... Arthur Wooster, BSC
Editor ... Robin Sales
Production Supervisor ... J Clive Hedges
1st Assistant Director ... Marc Jenny
2nd Assistant Director ... Sam Craddock
3rd Assistant Director ... Alejandro Sutherland
Unit Manager ... Christian Abomnes
Production Co-ordinator ... Liz Bunton
Script editor ... Gina Cronk
Script supervisor ... Elaine Matthews
London Contact ... Cindy Winter

Production Accountant ... Andy Hennigan
Camera Operator ... Martin Hume
Focus ... Sean Conner
Clapper/ Loader ... Helen Williams
Grip ... Philip Jones
Gaffers ... Yuri Nugis
... Eddie Knight
Sound Recordist ... Christian Wangler
Boom Operator ... St. Clair Davis
Art Directors ... Cliff Robinson, Philip Elton
Prop buyer ... Alison Stewart-Richardson
Props ... Colin Thurston
Make-up Supervisor ... Penny Smith
Make-up Artist ... Charmaine Gruhn
Make-up Assistant ... Fiona Clegg
Wardrobe Supervisor ... Steve Kirkby
Wardrobe Mistress ... Helen Khramova
Dubbing mixer ... Colin Martin
Assistant Editor ... Richard Milward
Stunt Co-ordinator/Horse Master ... Dinny Powell
Stunt co-ordinator ... Sasha Philatov
Special Effects Supervisor ... Goby Evitsky
Military Advisor ... Richard Moore
Armourer ... Tom Moriarty
Titles ... Baxter Hobbins Sides

FILMED IN THE UKRAINE WITH THE EAST-WEST
CREATIVE ASSOCIATION
Stepan Pojenian, Pavel Douvidson,
Igor Nossov, John Raymond, Tom Lasica,
Tatyana Shakhgeldian

SHARPE'S GOLD, SHARPE'S BATTLE and SHARPE'S SWORD

A CELTIC/ PICTURE PALACE PRODUCTION
FOR CARLTON UK PRODUCTIONS.
A CENTRAL PROGRAMME FOR ITV.
FILMED: AUGUST - DECEMBER 1994
TRANSMITTED: APRIL 1995

Director ... Tom Clegg
Producer ... Chris Burt
Executive producers ... Ted Childs
... Malcolm Craddock
... Muir Sutherland
Casting ... John and Ros Hubbard
... Lisa-Anne Porter
Music ... Dominic Muldowney,
... John Tams
Prouction Designer ... Andrew Mollo
Costume Designer ... Robin Fraser Paye
Editor ... Robin Sales
Director of Photography ... Chris O'Dell
Associate Producer ... Ray Frift
1st Assistant Director ... Michael Mallinson
2nd Assistant Director ... Sam Craddock
3rd Assistant Director ... Giles Butler
Unit Managers ... Alejandro Sutherland
... Tatyana Shakhgeldian
Production Co-ordinators ... Felicity Newton
... Lina Mercoulova
Script Editor ... Julia Ouston
Script Supervisor ... Marissa Cowell
London Contact ... Cindy Winter
Production Accountants ... Terry Connors
... Pat Harding
Camera Operator ... John Boulter
Focus Puller ... Charlie Palmer
Clapper/Loader ... Christian Abomnes
Grips ... Bob Dixon
... Yuri Komarov
Gaffer ... Yuri Nugis
Sound Recordist ... Christian Wangler
Boom Operator ... St. Clair Davis
Art Director ... Grant Montgomery
Set Dresser ... Bryony Foster
Stand-by Props ... Tony Ferguson
... Igor Guzun
Make-up artists ... Jacquetta Levon
Make-up assistant ... Fiona Clegg
Hairdresser ... Sano de Perpessac
Wardrobe Master ... Steve Kirkby
Wardrobe Mistress ... Helen Khramova
Wardrobe Assistant ... Lidia Schmidt
Dubbing Mixer ... Brian Saunders
Dubbing Editor ... Colin Chapman
Assistant Editor ... Jonathan Sales
Stunt Arrangers/Horsemasters ... Roy Street
... Sasha Philatov
Special Effects ... Goby Evitsky
Military Advisor ... Richard Moore
Armourer ... William J. Whitlam
Titles ... Baxter Hobbins Sides

FILMED IN THE UKRAINE WITH THE ASSISTANCE
OF THE EAST-WEST CREATIVE ASSOCIATION

Associate Producers (Ukraine) — Stepan Pojenian,
Igor Nossov, Pavel Douvidson

FILMED IN PORTUGAL WITH THE ASSISTANCE
OF ANIMEDIA
Patricia Vieira, Jose Correia, Fatima Correia

SHARPE'S REGIMENT, SHARPE'S SIEGE and SHARPE'S MISSION

A CELTIC/ PICTURE PALACE PRODUCTION
FOR CARLTON UK TELEVISION
A CARLTON UK PRODUCTION FOR ITV.
FILMED: AUGUST – DECEMBER 1995
TRANSMITTED: APRIL – MAY 1996

Producer ... Malcolm Craddock
Executive Producers ... Jonathan Powell
... Muir Sutherland
Director ... Tom Clegg
Casting ... John and Ros Hubbard
... Lisa-Anne Porter
Music ... Dominic Muldowney
... John Tams
Production Designer ... Andrew Mollo
Costume Designer ... Robin Fraser Paye
Supervising Editor ... Keith Palmer
Director of Photography ... Chris O'Dell
Production Manager (Turkey) ... Ali Akdeniz
Associate Producer ... Ray Frift
1st Assistant Director ... Michael Mallinson
2nd Assistant Director ... Sam Craddock
3rd Assistant Directors ... Giles Butler
... Gürcan Keltek
Unit Manager ... Alejandro Sutherland
Assistant Unit Manager (Turkey) ... Ahmet Uygun
Production Co-ordinators ... Felicity Newton
... Arzu Göknar
Location Managers ... Dennis Firminger
... Farouk Aksoy
Script Editor ... Rob Pursey
Script Supervisor ... Marissa Cowell
London Contact ... Cindy Winter
Producer's Assistant ... Katherine Hedderly
Istanbul Contact ... Sirma Bradley
Production Accountant ... Rex Mitchell
Assistant Accountants ... John Eccleston
... Muharrem Gulmez
... Charlotte Farrar
Camera Operator ... Martin Hume
Camera Assistant ... Yagiz Akaydin
Focus Puller ... Sean Connor
Clapper/Loader ... Christian Abomnes
Grip ... Bob Dixon
Gaffers ... Steve Costello, Ali Salim Yasar
Sound Recordists ... Christian Wangler
... Albert Bailey
Boom Operator ... St. Clair Davis
Art Directors ... Mike Joyce
... Robert Ide
... M. Ziya Ülkenciler
Assistant Art Director ... Selda Cicek
Draughtsman ... Stephen James Bream
Construction Manager ... Stuart Scott Watson
Set Decorator ... Alison Stewart-Richardson
Prop Master ... Peter Grant
Stand-by Props ... Colin Thurston
... Chris Brett
Prop Buyer (UK) ... Gina Cromwell
Chief make-up artist ... Jacquetta Levon
Make-up assistants ... Fiona Clegg
... Melissa Harding
... Leda Seril
... Sevinç Uçar
Hairdresser ... Julieanne Chapman
Assistant hairdressers ... Luisa Abel
... Davut Baskaya
... Kazim Caliskan
Wardrobe Master ... Russell Barnett
Editor ... Hugo Middleton
Assistant Editor ... Joe Illing
Dubbing Mixer ... Colin Martin
Stunt Arrangers/Horsemasters ... Dinny Powell
... Sasha Philatov
Special Effects ... Goby Evitsky
... Dmitro Stetsenko
... Oleg Trotsevsky
Military Advisor ... Richard Moore
Armourer ... William J. Whitlam
Casting (Turkey) ... Fatos Sevinç
... Seda Yılmaz
... Deniz Aksít
Catering ... Set Meals
Stills ... Tony Nutley
Unit Nurse ... Suzanne Freeborn
Titles ... Baxter Hobbins Sides

FILMED IN TURKEY WITH THE ASSISTANCE OF
THE EAST-WEST CREATIVE ASSOCIATION

FILMED IN TURKEY WITH THE ASSISTANCE
OF PANFILM

SHARPE'S REVENGE, SHARPE'S JUSTICE and SHARPE'S WATERLOO

A CELTIC/ PICTURE PALACE PRODUCTION
FOR CARLTON TELEVISION
A CARLTON PRODUCTION FOR ITV.
FILMED: AUGUST-DECEMBER 1996
TRANSMITTED: SPRING 1997

Director ... Tom Clegg
Executive Producers ... Jonathan Powell
... Muir Sutherland
Producer ... Malcolm Craddock
Casting ... John and Ros Hubbard
... Lisa-Anne Porter
Music ... Dominic Muldowney
... John Tams
Series Designer ... Andrew Mollo
Costume Designer ... Robin Fraser Paye
Supervising Editor ... Keith Palmer
Director of Photography ... Chris O'Dell
Production Supervisor ... John Kay
Production Manager (Turkey) ... Ali Akdeniz
1st Assistant Director ... Michael Mallinson
2nd Assistant Director ... Steve Robinson
3rd Assistant Directors ... Giles Butler
... Yagiz Akaydin
Production Co-ordinators ... Colleen Hughes
... Zeynep Ciftci
Location Managers ... Peter Cotton
... Alejandro Sutherland
... Bahadir Atay
Script Editor ... Rob Pursey
Script Supervisor ... Marissa Cowell
London Co-ordinator ... Cindy Winter
Producer's Assistant ... Katherine Hedderly
Istanbul Contact ... Demet Ozonur
Production Accountant ... Pauline Granby
Assistant Accountants ... Chris Tarry
... Erhan Ozogul
Camera Operator ... Lewis Foster
Focus Puller ... John Bailie
Clapper Loader ... Christian Abomnes
Grip ... Bob Dixon
Gaffers ... Barry Bell
... Ali Salim Yasar
Sound Recordist ... Christian Wangler
Boom Operator ... St. Clair Davies
Art Directors ... Mike Joyce
... Omer Ulkenciler
... Naslihan Zabci
Assistant Art Director ... Tristan Peatfield
Draughtsman ... Paul Westacott
Art Department Assistant ... Nick Mollo
Set Decorator ... Alison Stewart-Richardson
Prop Master ... Alan Bailey
Stand-by Props ... Colin Thurston
... Billy Edwards
... Dave Fisher
... Ali Ozguley
Prop-buyer (UK) ... Duncan Wheeler
Chief Make-up Artist ... Julieanne Chapman
Make-up Assistants ... Fiona Clegg
... Leda Seril
... Savinc Ucar
Hairdressers ... Laura Schiavo
... Murat Kara
Assistant Hairdressers ... Tamsin Dorling
... Zeki Bulut
Wardrobe Master ... Gordon Harmer
Wardrobe Mistress ... Elena Khramova
Wardrobe Assistant ... Lidia Schmidt
Assistant Editor ... Joe Illing
Dubbing Mixer ... Colin Martin
Horsemaster/ Stunt Arranger ... Gerard Naprous
Stunt Co-ordinator ... Sasha Philatov
Special Effects ... Josef Yvetskij
... Dima Stetsenkio
... Victor Voronoi
Military Adviser ... Richard Rutherford Moore
Armourer ... Tom Moriarty
Casting (Turkey) ... Deniz Aksit
... Devrim Nalci
Catering ... Set Meals
Stills ... Tony Nutley
Unit Nurse ... Suzanne Freeborn
Titles ... Baxter Hobbins Sides

FILMED IN TURKEY WITH THE ASSISTANCE OF
PANFILM